Fake Fear: America and China Relations

Xin Jiyan

Paths International Ltd

Preface

"We come nearest to the great when we are great in humility."

——Rabindranath Tagore

A fear, an inexplicable fear of China, is widespread in Washington.

There are claims that the Chinese have stolen jobs from the Americans, that the Chinese have stolen American technology and that China has dragged the world into a trap of debt. The world According to *China—Understanding the world China* seeks to create of 2049 when the People's Republic of China (PRC) Turns 100, by Bradley A. Thafer and John M. Friend, October 03, 2018 The National Interest.

What people will think in 2049 when they read the above-mentioned labels is perhaps the same as what they think today when they read the 2001 U.S. bestseller *The Coming Collapse of China.*[1] The book said: "The end of the modern Chinese state is near. The People's Republic has five years, perhaps ten, before it falls." Now 18 years after the book was published, what the book asserts may make many readers scratch their heads.

As everyone knows, Washington is currently besieged by hawkish policy-makers. In their eyes, China is indeed a cause for fear.

The age-old strategy of inciting fear and manipulating public opinion is still being adopted in the political arena of the world's most developed country.

Although China-bashing is not new, it is increasingly jeopardizing normal exchanges between China and the United States.

What the U.S. politicians are intentionally doing will widen the gap between the two countries. Meanwhile, it should not be overlooked that even in a globalized world with instant communication and information readily available on the worldwide web, fear and misunderstanding to some extent owe their origins to ignorance.

In the eyes of those industrialized and modern developed countries, the world is divided into the West and the rest. It seems hard for people who have long stayed at the top of the pyramid, such as G. W. Hegel, to accept the fact that a "static" country like China with a 5,000-year-old continuous civilization will catch up some day in its process of modernization.

Ignorance produces mystery and mystery fuels fear. Until today, the West still views China being veiled in "mystery."

"We mystified China," said Oscar-winner Malcolm Clarke at the premiere of his documentary *Better Angels* in Beijing in November 2018.[2]

China needs to be demystified, Martin Wolf, a Financial Times columnist, told a forum held by China's Tsinghua University in April 2018.

However, decreasing fear and unveiling the "mystery" of China needs efforts from both China and the West.

Western countries need to know not only Chinese history, but also Chinese reality. The philosophy and wisdom developed by the ancient Chinese as early as 2,000 years ago have been researched and acknowledged by the West. China's seeking modernization and new thoughts in modern times, however, have not been thoroughly studied.

For more than one hundred years, China has been endeavoring to learn how to get along with the West.

During a century of humiliation dated back to 1840, China lagged behind and was vulnerable to attacks. China once feared the West. Perhaps Westerners cannot completely understand the vicissitudes behind "Western powers" — an expression that has been written into Chinese history textbooks.

People can care about etiquette and pay attention to honor and disgrace only after they have ample food and clothing. From standing up to getting rich, China spent just decades achieving its goal and it is still pursuing its dream of becoming strong. The Chinese built roads to get rich and built walls to stop war. China has striven to survive, to develop and not to be a dependent state while sticking to its own development path in order to earn equality and respect. The acts of modern China owe their origins to Chinese history and culture.

But China, a country with a long history and a late-comer in modernization and globalization, is still not eloquent. Chinese stories that have inherited the more-than-4000-year-old hieroglyphics are not that easy to understand. China needs a new narrative and time for the world to understand it.

China is quickening its pace to catch up and is learning to innovate. The best contribution China has made to the world is solving its problems within its territory. In the path of exploration the People's Republic of China has followed, especially within the last 40 years of reform and opening-up, China has created a miracle of development and modernization. The narrative of this miracle is very much grounded in reality.

If Americans know the price China has paid for its success, they will admire China instead of fearing it because they will find that the price would have been too high for themselves to pay, said Clarke.

It is hard to understand the complex diversity in China from a traditional Western perspective. The legitimacy of the Chinese political system is because China is a civilization-state.[3]

On the global stage of the 21st century, the actors have changed. A new world needs a new world view. The centuries-old viewpoint of major-country conflict and power politics does not conform to the new times any more. The notion of either China-West or South-North conflict should remain confined to historical textbooks.

To deconstruct an imaginary China and dispel its inexplicable fear, the United States and the West also need to engage in some self-reflection.

Western philosophies say that who destroys you is not the enemy you face, but the devil in your heart. "If you treat China as an enemy, China will become an enemy."[4] The United States should not attempt to "stand in the way of China's legitimate economic growth."[5]

In 2008, a global financial crisis broke out and the "financial weapons of mass destruction" put the United States in the spotlight again. Primary capitalism has collapsed from a moral perspective. It has creatively destroyed irrational prosperity and let humanity face reality. It also let China see the U.S. and Western governance in crisis.[6] The Chinese who once worshipped the West began to look at the United States and the world in a more rational way.

The Austrian economist Peter Schumpeter points out, crisis is the process by which economic life adapts itself to the new economic conditions. China and the United States need a more equal notion and mutual respect.

As China has always been a champion of world peace, a contributor to global development and a defender of the international order, people with "better angles" inside their heart will believe that China in 2049 will not threaten the United States and the world.

In 2049, the United States is expected to be the only major developed country with an increasing young population. A new survey showed that immigrants in the United States have increased at a rate faster than most people imagined and the U.S. birthrate is surprisingly increasing. With the current trend, until 2050, the U.S. population will increase to around 550 million, while those countries affected by the aging of their populations have to distribute more resources to the elderly.

In the past decades, China-U.S. cooperation has created a global supply chain that has benefited billions of people around the world. But the chain can be ruptured in a flash and this is what should really make the world afraid.

As frenemies, China and the United States can be pillars of the international system.[7] Both the two great nations need to be admired, not feared.

In an inter-dependent world, China and the United States need to cooperate to coexist on an increasingly crowded and fragile planet. We have national rights but also global responsibilities. How we advance depends on our patience and whether we can learn to listen to others.

China has, since ancient times, been an exponent of harmony in diversity. Balancing the centrifugal and centripetal forces, a new global contract is forming. It is believed that the two great nations can find a way to get along with each other so as to create a better future for mankind.

[1] Gordon G. Chang, *The Coming Collapse of China*, Penguin Random House, 2001.
[2] Malcolm Clarke, at the Beijing premiere of Better Angels, Nov. 24, 2018.
[3] Martin Jacques, *When China Rules the World: The End of the Western World and Birth of a New Global Order*, Penguin Books, 2012, pp.241-293.
[4] Joseph Nye, *Is the American Century Over* (Chinese version), Beijing United Publishing, 2016 Maybe include where the book was published? Page number needed.
[5] Raghuram Rajan, "Rather than attempting to stand in the way of China's legitimate economic growth, western efforts might be better focused on negotiating a new global order, while creating an external environment which does not prevent internal Chinese political change." Financial Times, December 5, 2018, https://www.ft.com/content/e881336a-f4b4-11e8-938a-543765795f99
[6] Andrew Sheng, *From Asian to Global Financial Crisis: An Asian Regulator's View of Unfettered Finance in the 1990s and 2000s*, Cambridge University Press, 2009.
[7] Jeffrey A. Bader, *Both China, U.S. can be pillars of international system*, December 2018, http://www.sohu.com/a/279688546_260616

Contents

Chapter Four Self Changing and the Myth to Change China / 65

Chapter Five "Empress of China" and Statue of Liberty / 91

Chapter Six Fake News and Real Gaps / 107

Chapter One

Chinese Dream & American Dream

"Today is only one day in all the days that will ever be. But what will happen in all the other days that ever come can depend on what you do today."

—Ernest Hemingway

"Chinese dream and American dream, can the dreams dream together?"

This question was asked on March 24, 2018 at a seminar at the annual China Development Forum held at the Diaoyutai State Guesthouse in Beijing. Stephen Roach, a senior fellow at Yale University's Jackson Institute for Global Affairs, known for advocating effective communication between China and the United States, posed the question to the lecturer on the stage, Robert Schiller, Nobel laureate in economics in 2013. The audience burst into laughter, however, Roach did not bat an eyelash.

Just two days ago, U.S. President Donald Trump signed the presidential memorandum to announce that in response to China's so-called violation of U.S. intellectual property rights, tariffs would be imposed on up to 60 billion U.S. dollars of imports from China in accordance with Section 301 of the

Trade Act of 1974. Not long ago, Trump also formally signed proclamations to impose steel and aluminum tariffs on its major trading partners in the world. With increasing protectionism and deteriorating trade relations between China and the United States, the term "trade war" has spread rapidly in the international field of public opinion.

As an economist who has been dealing with Chinese issues for a long time, Roach posed a question that reflects unprecedented anxiety about China even among rational scholars in the United States, while their Chinese academic peers are also worried.

The relations between the United States and China are at a crossroads.[1] The cooperation model between the two countries needs to be reconsidered.[2]

Dreams are ideas for the future. Are the dreams of the two great countries "concerted" or "dangerous" to each other? The answer to this question is related to the future well-being of all mankind.

The term "Chinese Dream" was inspired by the concept of the American Dream. It is in recent years that the Chinese Dream has become widely recognized in the world. More and more American scholars have begun to try to interpret its meaning, while regrettably, in the eyes of some American hawks toward China, the Chinese Dream may be a nightmare.

In the Chinese narrative, the Chinese dream is the great rejuvenation of the Chinese nation, representing the longing of the Chinese people for better lives. Why was this simple and reasonable wish translated into the above-mentioned demonized concepts in the Western world, especially in the United States?

I. Popular Narrative: The Ignored Rising Influence

Each March in the first week after the two sessions of China's top legislative and advisory bodies, the Chinese government's top leadership meets with hundreds of leaders from international institutions, academia and companies. They gather at the Diaoyutai State Guesthouse in Beijing for the China Development Forum, a state-level international forum organized by the Development Research Center of the State Council. With the objective of "Engaging with the World for Common Prosperity," the forum has been held for 18 consecutive years since its inauguration in 2000 and has become an important platform for China to learn from the world and interact with international thinkers. It is worthwhile to note that more than half of the distinguished foreign guests at the forum are from the United States.

At the forum in 2018, Robert Schiller, an expert on behavioral economics, pointed out an important issue that has been overlooked: the impact of popular narratives on China-U.S. relations is growing. Schiller, who accurately predicted the dot-com bubble with the book *Irrational Exuberance*, found that currently there are two very popular narratives between China and the U.S. — "Chinese Dream" and "trade war".

He said that the term "trade war" became popular for the first time during the Great Depression of the 1930s. According to the word frequency analysis, the "trade war" narrative has reached unprecedented popularity. Its viral spread is largely due to the fact that President Trump as a real master of broadcast rules on Internet platforms is truly willing to take the risk of starting a trade war.

Regarding the Chinese Dream, Schiller found historical facts proving the word was first used in the ancient poem written by painter and poet Zheng Sixiao in the Southern Song Dynasty in the 13th century. But the concept may not have become popular again without Chinese President Xi Jinping's promotion of this concept, Schiller said. In many countries, people are also talking about their own dreams, but similar efforts won't necessarily go viral. Former French President Francois Hollande has proposed the term "French Dream," but it never caught on and most French people are not familiar with this concept.

In the era of rapid development of high-tech, all countries in the world, developing or developed, will face an unprecedented new variable and challenge in international exchanges, which is brought about by popular narratives in the context of instant messaging. Considering the fact that one can access the Internet anytime through mobile devices, the rapid popularity of a keyword advocated by Chinese leaders can be attributed to modern communication technology. Yet a more important reason is that China is at the center of such a narrative.

Even the most hypercritical Western observers won't deny that the overall rise of developing countries in the past 100 years has been one of the greatest success stories in the history of human development. In this process, China as the world's largest developing country has undoubtedly garnered the most attention.

In the past 40 years, more than 700 million Chinese people have been lifted out of poverty; China's total economic output has increased by more than 40 times; the middle-income group in China has reached 400 million, the largest around the globe ... No one could have successfully predicted China's development story since its reform and opening-up in 1978. The rapid accumulation of material wealth and explosive social progress have confused and intrigued many observers outside China. What will the Chinese Dream mean for the world by 2049 when the country celebrates its centennial anniversary?

With incredible vitality, China with its 5,000-year-old civilization is still on the path of modernization, facing more and more globally trending narratives and interpretations from different perspectives.

Those who have negative interpretations of the Chinese Dream often overlook or do not understand the complex historical context behind it.

II. Some Historic Moments Covered in Dust

People are prisoners of ideas,[3] while ideas live in concepts and expressions.

As opposed to the United States, which has a brief history of over 240 years, China always had to deal with its historical burden of a hundred years of humiliation.

"America will march along that skyline." In 1924, the sculptor Gutzon Borglum said so to the state historian Doane Robinson when he saw Mount Rushmore in the U.S. state of South Dakota. After 14 years of construction, the sculptures feature the 60-foot-high (18 meter-high) heads of four U.S. presidents, namely George Washington, Thomas Jefferson, Theodore Roosevelt and Abraham Lincoln. The "President Hill" represents the United States' first 150 years of history and has become a symbol of the American spirit.

If there was a time machine, perhaps one would have a new understanding of the different vicissitudes represented by the Chinese Dream and the American Dream, after comparing the different development paths of China and the United States in the same historic moments.

Historic Moment I

In 1789, General George Washington, who led the Continental Army in the American Revolutionary War, became the first president of the United States. At the same time in Europe, the British industrial revolution was in the ascendant and the French Revolution was about to erupt. The independence of the United States, a new country with only more than three million people and an adherent of isolationism, did not attract the attention of the Qing Empire lying in the East.

In the same year, China had been under the rule of the Qianlong Emperor for 41 years. The huge empire possessed one third of the world's wealth, with nearly 300 million people living in peace and prosperity. However, the habit of self-sufficiency, conservatism and increasing self-satisfaction formed in a millennium was pushing the empire to the edge of an abyss full of unknowns. The fatalistic cycle of history emerged in the Qing Dynasty, but it remained oblivious and content in its retreat. It was not until the First Opium War that the empire finally woke up, startled.

Historic Moment II

In 1803, the third president of the United States Thomas Jefferson bought Louisiana, basically another United States, from France at a total price of 15 million U.S. dollars, which is less than three cents per acre (seven dollars per square kilometer). The Louisiana Purchase more than doubled the territory of the United States at the time. At that time, Jefferson's old rival Alexander Hamilton had only one year left to live. The fierce debate between the two American founding fathers has since laid the foundation for the country's ideological theories.

At the same time in Asia, the Jiaqing Emperor, who had been in power for eight years, escaped an assassination. A few months later, he accepted the request of Gia Long, first Emperor of the Nguyen Dynasty of Vietnam, to join the Imperial Chinese Tributary System. Both the Jiaqing Emperor and the Qing Dynasty remained in a state of systemic complacency.

Historic Moment III

In 1861, the Civil War broke out in the United States and brought along the emancipation of slaves, making the United States of America united again. The 16th president, Abraham Lincoln, gave a short five-minute speech at Gettysburg, Pennsylvania. Since then, the principle of "the government of the people, by the people, for the people" has spread throughout the world.

The same year in Qing-dynasty China, the Xianfeng Emperor died and Empress Dowager Cixi started her actual rule that would last for more than 40 years. The year of 1861 is also the 10th year of the Taiping Revolution, a massive rebellion started by the Taiping Heavenly Kingdom under Hong Xiuquan in a bid to overthrow the Qing Dynasty. The rebellion, which shocked the Western countries, was called by Karl Marx "a people's war"[4], as "outsiders often act rudely against the inherently mild Chinese". The energy demonstrated by the Chinese when fighting against foreign invaders astounded countries around the world. However, in the 19th century, China still retained the characteristics of an absolute monarchy, a stable society and a culture that clearly lacks individuality, as described by Ralph Waldo Emerson, who was called the American Confucius by U.S. President Lincoln.[5]

Historic Moment IV

In September 1901, the 42-year-old Theodore Roosevelt became the 26th president of the United States. In the five years before his inauguration, the total economy of the United States ranked first in the world. The energetic and youngest U.S. president ever domestically established a resource protection policy and fair trade bill, while externally pursuing Monroeism and expansionism, which greatly advanced the modernization of the young country.

Meanwhile in China, the year 1901 represents the start of the final decade of the monarchy. In September, the Qing Empire was subjected to great humiliation and signed the Boxer Protocol with 11 Western countries. The signing showed that Chinese society was completely reduced to semi-colonial and semi-feudal status, and the Chinese people suffered for nearly half a century. It was not until 1949 that the 28-year-old Communist Party of China led the founding of the People's Republic of China, bringing about a dramatic change in Chinese people's mindset and life. Nevertheless, the shame that had lasted for more than a century since the Opium War is still deeply engrained in the memory of all the Chinese.

On the morning of Nov. 11, 2018, the 100th anniversary of the end of

World War I was held at the Arc de Triomphe in Paris. The ceremony was attended by French President Emmanuel Macron, U.S. President Donald Trump, Russian President Vladimir Putin, German Chancellor Angela Merkel, as well as dozens of monarchs, presidents and prime ministers from countries in Europe, Africa, the Middle East and other regions in the world. All stood to commemorate the moment when the fire of war was finally eliminated in Europe, and to pay tribute to the approximately ten million soldiers who were killed in the war.

There was no Chinese leader attending the international commemorative ceremony gathering about 70 state leaders. That is because in the eyes of Westerners, the role of China in WWI, a war that affected Europe's destiny 100 years ago, was confined to that of Chinese workers serving the Western Front. Nevertheless, an interesting detail at the ceremony was captured by the Western media. According to the Guardian, Chinese-American cellist Yo-Yo Ma played the Sarabande from J.S. Bach's Cello Suite No. 5 near the eternal flame at the Arc de Triomphe. While the melody was playing, teenagers read excerpts of letters in French, English and Chinese written by people bearing witness to the end of the war, among whom was a Chinese worker.

One is bullied if one lags behind; having a feeling of shame gives rise to courage. The Chinese people know that they are the latecomers in the world and keep pursuing the human modernization process. However, even now, Westerners probably still cannot understand the efforts the once humiliated Chinese people would like to make to get rid of their role of the underdog. The bloody memories have been turned into drums inspiring generations of Chinese people to pursue the ambition of making China a powerful country again.

Although China has already become world's second largest economy, its gross domestic product (GDP) per capita still ranks around No. 70 in the world, which makes it still a developing country. Meanwhile, rationalists know that with a heavy historical burden, even if China could become the No.1 economy in the world by 2049, it will not seek world hegemony as some Westerners believe.

However, in the global contrast between countries' modernization and modernity level, China, like all other countries and regions in the world, has long been under the influence of the United States. According to Chinese scholar Wang Yiwei, China has actually learned a lot from the United States, not by completely copying but by finding local equivalents to the U.S. counterparts, for example, by creating the term "Chinese Dream" with reference to the "American Dream".

Thomas Jefferson once said during the era when France was a powerful force in the world, "every man has two countries—his own and France," while nowadays everyone also has two countries—their own and the United States. American culture seems so ubiquitous that everyone seems to have a virtual United States in his or her mind; the United States is so overwhelming a power that people around the world are paying close and constant attention to American politicians just like heeding politics in their motherlands. Along with this kind of acquaintance with the United States is a growing sense of helplessness. Everyone in the world is involved in American culture and policy, and in this sense everyone feels that they have become American citizens.[6]

The United States is anxious about China because it overestimates it. The difficult part for China is that it has suddenly been pushed to a higher platform and has been given higher expectations by many parties, but it has not fully adapted to this. Just like one standing on a stage with one's back facing the audience, China thinks that it is still a spectator, China's former Deputy Minister of Foreign Affairs Fu Ying said. China is trying to learn how to become a world citizen and play a bigger role in the international arena, but the process takes time.[7]

Henry Kissinger once said that he personally thinks that China doesn't have the ambition of replacing the United States; it only hopes to gain the respect it deserves. As China becomes more affluent and powerful, its desire to be respected will be even stronger, he added.[8]

III. Two-Way Knowledge Deficit

"This expo reflects an important signal that we welcome: the importance of import. It reminds us of an important fact, that trade is not a zero-sum game, not export is good and import is bad," said Roberto Azevedo, chief of the World Trade Organization on November 5, 2018 at the opening ceremony of China's first International Import Expo in Shanghai.

In his opinion, the expo can be seen as a new contribution made by China to 21st-century world trade, as the world is not fully aware of the changes of concepts which used to be treated as common sense.

For more than a century and a half since the Opium War, China has seen the net inflow of Western experiences with a huge knowledge deficit. The desire for knowledge in the outside world, especially in the Western developed countries, has affected the life of the Chinese people.

In the 40 years since the reform and opening-up, China has been learning and catching up. While striving to achieve modernization, China has become increasingly modernized and gradually began to contribute more and more modern knowledge it has gained by itself to the world. However, regarding the perception of China, there is still a two-way knowledge deficit between the outside world and China itself.

Overall, in the international knowledge and information data base, modern knowledge originating from Chinese mainland has always been scarce, let alone its systematization and completeness ... The external "information deficit" about China is quite serious. The lack of information often misguides the media and the public to jump to the wrong conclusions regarding the contemporary China, and politicians build their views on the basis of incomplete information.[9]

The West looks at apples (the West) to discuss oranges (China), Singapore-based scholar Zheng Yongnian said.[10] However, until today, China itself cannot answer the question of "What is China".[11]

"An important generational milestone has been passed without drawing attention to itself," said Douglas H. Paal, vice president for studies at the Carnegie Endowment for International Peace. "Across the American government, in every agency and regardless of party identification, those with experience with pre-reform China have retired and been replaced by much younger officials..." But the new generation of U.S. officials in charge of the government doesn't really know about China, he said.[12]

Ordinary people in the United States do not understand what the Chinese people are thinking, nor about their daily life. They just know that the Chinese people are getting richer and richer, and China has become a richer and stronger country, more and more like the United States, Kissinger told Chinese officials who paid him a visit in the United States in June 2014.[13]

Humans have a fear of the unknown. Facing an increasingly powerful China, the new generation of U.S. policy makers, who lack both practices proven in the history of Sino-U.S. relations and understanding of the real thoughts of the Chinese people, often come up with fierce words and deeds against China. The Chinese Dream is also being regarded suspiciously.

The United States, which has been a world superpower for many years, seems to be losing its superiority when facing a prospering China.

"We lost their respect," U.S. Republican presidential candidate Donald Trump said in a speech on foreign policy at the Center for the National

Interests on April 27, 2016. It is in this world-famous speech that Trump put forward the popular and enduring narrative of "American First".

Perhaps the root of anxiety and fear caused by losing respect should be found within oneself.

"Many Americans seem concerned that their country is not as respected as they believed it was," said former World Bank President Robert Zoellick at the end of 2016, worrying about the increasingly serious populism in the United States.[14]

Robert Hormats, former undersecretary of state under the Obama administration and now Vice Chairman of the New York-based consulting firm Kissinger Associates, has frankly admitted that China is becoming more and more competitive in the high-tech sector. China and the United States have to answer the question of who is No.1 in the global high-tech field, a question the United States has never had to face before.[15]

Hormats said Americans have long believed and insisted that only Western democratic institutions can bring prosperity and development, but China has become a counterexample. The Chinese government has shown it is better than the U.S. government in certain aspects such as emergency and disaster relief, and the fact has blown Americans away. They need time to digest and deal with it.[16]

The worrying fact is that in the U.S. decision-making and academic circles, some outdated theories still occupy international relations issues due to the long-term unresolved challenge of information deficit.

"This being inherently a world of opposing interests and of conflict among them, moral principles can never be fully realized, but must at best be approximated through the ever temporary balancing of interests and the ever precarious settlement of conflicts."[17] The thought of Hans J. Morgenthau is still regarded as a standard in the United States.

Wang Jisi, a professor at the Institute of International and Strategic Studies at China's Peking University, believes that after the Cold War, especially in the 21st century, inter-state politics has been changed to and become an integral part of world politics or global politics.[18]

In the era of Morgenthau, the leading part of international politics was the two tragic world wars, followed by the U.S.-USSR Cold War which many feared back then could trigger World War III. The gloom of nuclear war between major powers only began to dissipate during the disintegration of the Soviet Union, which also reduced the possibility of large-scale military conflict.

The in-depth informatization and globalization unprecedentedly accelerated the speed, as well as enlarged the breadth and depth of the world's interconnection. What a country, a city, or even an ordinary person does can instantly become an international hot spot attracting the world's attention. However, even in this context, research on international issues seriously lags behind.

Machiavellianism, conspiracy theories ... Scholars on Chinese issues in the U.S. and the Western English-speaking world are still willing to interpret ancient Chinese philosophical thoughts with mysticism.[19] However, they rarely carry out in-depth studies into the contemporary Chinese mainstream political thoughts, a combination of traditional culture, Marxist philosophy and advanced culture in the world.

More than 100 years ago, the Chinese people began to look at and interact with the world, but nowadays it is the world that needs to look more clearly at China, to understand how a 5,000-year-old civilization can renew its vitality. At the same time, China needs to bid farewell to the historical tragedy of a hundred years of humiliation and deal with the future of China from civilizational perspective.[20]

The paradox of the United States is that it is both the most admired country and one of the most criticized countries in the world.[21]

For China, being misunderstood in the world remains its test of endurance, while the process also entails its growth and progress.

IV. Family & Country: An Unexceptional Chinese Dream

There is a "Chinese exception theory" among U.S. scholars in Chinese studies in the United States: Some American scholars believe that the Chinese Dream is an exception that is difficult to understand. Just like the way Chinese people feel about family and country, there is the same mysterious feeling in the notion of Chinese Dream.

"When one family becomes humane, the whole country will be stimulated to become humane. When one family becomes easy to get along with, all the people in the country are stimulated to become easy to get along with." The excerpt from the Chinese ancient classic the *Great Learning* or *Daxue* shows the strong relations between family and country in Chinese thought. The country can be treated as a big family, while the family is a country in miniature. China's modern history of humiliation makes its people more firmly believe in the dialectical relationship between a country's power and peace and its people's well-being.

A country's dreams help its people look forward to the future.

On the morning of Nov. 29, 2012, Chinese President Xi Jinping and other members of the Standing Committee of the Political Bureau of the Communist Party of China Central Committee visited the National Museum for the exhibition Road of Rejuvenation, where Xi cited three famous verses to describe China's yesterday, today and tomorrow:

"Idle boast the strong pass is a wall of iron."

"But man's world if mutable, seas become mulberry fields."

"A time will come when a breeze breaks waves, bringing fair weather (so that one could set a cloud for sails cross the blue oceans)."

With his country's future in mind, Xi remarked on the struggle for the realization of the Chinese Dream during his visit. He said: "Everyone has an ideal, ambition and dream. We are now all talking about the Chinese Dream. In my opinion, achieving the rejuvenation of the Chinese nation has been the greatest dream of the Chinese people since the advent of modern times. This dream embodies the long-cherished hope of several generations of the Chinese people, gives expression to the overall interests of the Chinese nation and the Chinese people, and represents the shared aspiration of all the sons and daughters of the Chinese nation."[22]

Li Junru, a communist theorist and former vice president of the Party School of the CPC Central Committee, believes that the idea of the Chinese Dream builds a bridge between the CPC and the people, one that connects the party's proposition with the people's wish. This most contagious and resounding term could easily be understood by the Chinese people. The ideal can enhance cohesion, and organize and mobilize people to devote themselves to life and work.[23]

What does the Chinese Dream have to do with us? This is a question asked by the international community when faced with China's rising influence.

The Chinese Dream is to strive for a peaceful international environment for one's own development, and simultaneously use one's own development to maintain and promote world peace and common development. This is the foundation of China's peaceful development path, and also reflects the essential requirements of socialism with Chinese characteristics, Li said. According to the theorist, the Chinese Dream also emphasizes equal consideration for the overall international and domestic situations, and asks for perseverance of every party involved in international relations and issues to pursue in all the dream of peace, development, cooperation and international harmony.[24]

From a global perspective, people's understanding of the American Dream is relatively clear, which is the pursuit of individual wealth and success and the strategy of America First at the national level.

Compared with the political system, ideology and cultural traditions of the United States, the Chinese Dream may indeed be an exception in the eyes of Americans. However, there is no natural difference between the Chinese Dream and American Dream considering their final goal, which is to reduce the gap between the rich and the poor, improve market efficiency, promote social equity and improve the well-being of all people. The only difference is that China believes the way to realize its dream should be changed considering the 21st-century reality of a deeply interconnected globe.

China has never sent soldiers outside its borders for resources, colonized other countries, or formed political blocs to confront others in order to expand. China is instead participating in the world market with mutually beneficial competition, gaining resources and technology needed for its industrialization and modernization by peaceful means, and cooperating with other countries in international political platforms such the United Nations. Through development, China gave up the outdated rule of fighting for resources during a country's rapid industrialization, and the Cold War mentality of rejecting cooperation because of ideological differences. China depends on its own reform and opening-up, and is independently building a nation that is economically and politically powerful. Making all efforts without seeking hegemony or depending on another country is the characteristic of Chinese socialism.[25]

China is creating a new social, economic and political system. Its political model may prove that capitalism, the so-called end of history, is only one stage of human history, according to world-known U.S. futurist John Naisbitt.[26]

Most countries in the world would like to maintain good relations with the United States and China at the same time, making it impossible to form an anti-China alliance, said Prof. Joseph Nye of Harvard University, who coined the term "soft power".[27]

V. Shared Dream: A Delicate Dance

"China is not 'rise,' but 'reemergence,'" Charlene Barshefsky, former U.S. Trade Representative, once told the media. "The U.S. and China MUST cooperate. But it is a delicate dance."

Before the 2010 China-U.S. Strategic and Economic Dialogue was held, C. Fred Bergsten, director emeritus of the Peterson Institute for International Economics, a think tank based in Washington D.C., said that any country in its growth stage should strive on its own for power, as no country with vested interests is willing to share or relinquish.

As "trade war" has become the current international popular narrative, China and the United States, as two major powers on their journey of pursuing their dreams, need to gradually adapt to each other through new ways of strategical interaction.

Western scholars on diplomacy who adhere to realism would think that a military conflict between China and the United States would not be surprising. John Mearsheimer, a professor of political science at the University of Chicago, thinks that it is inevitable for countries to fight for the No.1 rank in an anarchic world of big power politics, a view which is echoed by Harvard professor Graham Allison, who believes that war would often come along.[28]

In fact, China has been actively seeking changes, a fact which has already been discovered by those wise observers.

"China is a young country with old history," Michel Haese, a German who has been living in China's Shenzhen for a long time, said. He has come to the conclusion that China is striving every day to change itself, speed up its opening-up and adapt itself more quickly to the world, which can be seen in its anti-corruption efforts and the building of ecological civilization.

The world needs to see China's development style from a new perspective. The world must understand that some unchangeableness is rooted in China's long history and update its knowledge in order to better understand China.

"China is not 'ours' to make or remake. It belongs to the Chinese and to nobody else ... China's political organization is likely to remain different from the west's indefinitely."[29] "The Chinese, in other words, still refused to see the Westerners as the Westerners saw themselves."[30]

"After going through 5,000 years of trials and tribulations, China is still here! Looking ahead, China will always be here to stay!"[31]

China has two main characteristics, which are its concept of a civilization-state and its experience as a tributary system. "China should not primarily be seen as a nation state but rather as a civilization-state. The implications of this are far-reaching: It is simply not possible to regard China as like, or equivalent to, any other state." China should be treated as a civilization-state at first, and then a nation state. One should understand the complex diversity of China, and sticking to the traditional Western concept cannot help understand China's political system. The legitimacy of China's politic system lies at the root of it being a civilization-state.[32]

China and the United States should manage crises skillfully and should continue to cooperate, as bilateral relations should be maintained not only to the benefits of the two countries.

"Cold war or not, this strategic conflict looks deep and enduring. The U.S. must reset chilling rhetoric on rise of China. Maintaining the stability of the world economy and managing climate change will be impossible without co-operation with China," Martin Wolf, British economics journalist and chief economics commentator at the *Financial Times*, said.[33]

Such a view also won applause in the United States.

"That is the most essential ingredient if America is to compete with China smartly, now and into the future—with favor not fear, with confidence not caution," said former U.S. Treasury Secretary Henry Paulson. China and the United States altogether account for 40 percent of the world's economy and contribute more than 50 percent of global economic growth, which makes it possible for the two countries to "work in complementary ways" in strategic interactions.[34] This will create the most profound impact on the world.

The struggle, progress, innovation and development of the United States have always been admired by China, which aims to learn from United States. A country with less than 5 percent of the world population accounts for 25 percent of the global gross domestic product (GDP). Anyone can attain everything he or she wants through working and creating: Such an "American Dream" however is impossible in other countries of the world. In China and India, with 37 percent of world population in total, resources and the environment do not allow their populations to achieve such a dream. China has to develop and at the same time cope with the problems of global warming and environmental sustainability. As there is no universal reform model nor development model, every country should develop based on its own national conditions.

"Before the second half of the twentieth century the West enjoyed a de facto monopoly of modernity. We are witnessing the birth of a world of multiple and competing modernities. This will be a quite new and novel feature of the twenty-first century, ushering in an era of what I characterize as contested modernity. Given that China promises to be so inordinately powerful and different, it is difficult to resist the idea that in time its rise will herald the birth of a new international order."[35]

It is dangerous to try to replicate containment thinking in the Cold War theory. As former Australian Prime Minister Kevin Rudd has said, "Some U.S. strategic planners may be considering further reorienting U.S. China policy from strategic competition toward full-blooded containment and comprehensive economic decoupling, George Kennan's famous 'Long Telegram' of 1946 and his 'X' article on 'The Sources of Soviet Conduct,' published in *Foreign Affairs* the following year, are worth a careful rereading.

"Kennan argued that if properly contained the Soviet Union would likely break up under the weight of its internal pressures. It would be a heroic assumption, however, that holds that in a new Cold War, the Chinese system would collapse under the weight of its own internal contradictions should a similar policy be applied. It might. But the size of China's domestic economy, the extent of its continuing economic engagement with the rest of the non-U.S. world, together with the new technologies of political control now available to an authoritarian state, should give those who think that China will turn out just like the Soviet Union pause for thought."[36]

The method of labeling should not be used when dealing with the complicated relationship between China and the United States. Only through calm and objective analyses of the differences between the two countries, creative thinking on methods to bridge differences and make mutual compromises, could China and the U.S. avoid uncontrolled situations or even war bred by populism and disputes.[37]

Wolf reminded that the West should "have confidence in our values of freedom and democracy. Understand that it is on the creation of new ideas that we depend, not the protection of old ones. That in turn depends on freedom of inquiry and openness to the best talent from around the world. If western countries lose these, they will lose the future. Our enemy is not China. As the greatest U.S. president of the 20th century declared: 'The only thing we have to fear is fear itself.'"[38]

The world needs a new script. Its new generation should be able to go beyond the traditional thinking of a major country seeking hegemony and find a connection between the Chinese Dream and the American Dream.

[1] Henry M. Paulson, Jr. *The United States and China at a Crossroads,* Speech at Asia Society, November 16, 2018.

[2] Henry Kissinger, Speech at Bloomberg New Economy Forum, Singapore, November 6, 2018.

[3] Qian Mansu, *Emerson and China: the Reflection of Individualism*, Orient Publishing House, May 2018, p. 13.

[4] Karl Max, *Marx and Engels On China*, People's Publishing, March, 1950, p. 87.

[5] Qian Mansu, *Emerson and China: the Reflection of Individualism*,Orient Publishing House, May 2018, p. 230.

[6] John Micklethwait, Adrian Wooldridge, *The Right Nation: Conservative Power in America*, Penguin Books, 2005.

[7] Fu Ying, *See the World*, Citic Publishing House, June 2018, pp. 134-135.

[8] Fu Ying, *See the World*, Citic Publishing House, June 2018, p. 136.

[9] Fu Ying, *Tell China's Stories Properly and Improve International Communication*, People's Daily, March 12, 2018.

[10] Zheng Yongnian, *The Rebuilding of China's Knowledge*, Orient Publishing House, March 2018.

[11] Zheng Yongnian, *The Rebuilding of China's Knowledge*, Orient Publishing House, March 2018, p.13.

[12] Douglas Paal, "How the New Generation in Washington to Solve U.S.-China Trade Dispute, Taiwan and South China Sea Issues", *South China Morning Post*, Hong Kong, November 2018.

[13] Fu Ying, *See the World*, Citic Publishing House, June 2018, p. 135.

[14] Robert Zoellick, "After Obama: Future of U.S. Foreign Policy", *Financial Times*, October 19, 2016.

[15] Robert D. Hormats: *America Worries Not the Present, But the Future*, Wechat of Chongyang Financial School of Renmin University, November 18, 2018.

[16] Robert D. Hormats: *America Worries Not the Present, But the Future*, Wechat of Chongyang Financial School of Renmin University, November18, 2018.

[17] Hans J. Morgenthau, revised by Kenneth W. Thompson and W. David Cliton,

Politics Among Nations: The Struggle for Power and Peace, 7th Edition, McGraw-Hill Companies, Inc. 2005.

[18] Hans J. Morgenthau, revised by Kenneth W. Thompson and W. David Cliton, *Politics Among Nations: The Struggle for Power and Peace*, 7th Edition, 2005 by the McGraw-Hill Companies, Inc. Peking University Publishing House, November 2006, foreword by Wang Jisi.

[19] Francois Jollien, translated by Janet Lloyd, *A Treatise on Efficacy: Between Western and Chinese Thinking,* University of Hawaii Press (April 30, 2004), Inc. Beijing University Publishing House, November 2013; Roger T. Ames, *The Art of Rulership: A Study of Ancient Chinese Political Thought,* SUNY Press 1994.

[20] Zheng Yongnian, *The Revival of China's Civilization*, Orient Publishing House, March 2018.

[21] John Micklethwait, Adrian Wooldridge, *The Right Nation: Conservative Power in America*, Penguin Books, Reprint edition (May 31, 2005), Citic Publishing House, April 2014, p.16.

[22] *People's Daily*, November 30, 2012.

[23] Li Junru, *In Pursuit of the Chinese Dream*, p. 2, p. 4, Foreign Languages Press, 2015.

[24] Li Junru, *In Pursuit of the Chinese Dream*, p. 67, Foreign Languages Press, 2015.

[25] Li Junru, *In Pursuit of the Chinese Dream*, p. 79, Foreign Languages Press, 2015.

[26] John Naisbitt and Doris Naisbitt, *China's Megatrends: Eight Pillars of the New Society*, Jilin Publishing Group, September 2009, p. 4.

[27] Joseph Nye JR., *Is the American Century Over?* Polity, 2015.

[28] Graham Allison, *Destined For War: Can America and China Escape Thucydides's Trap?* Houghton Mifflin Harcourt, Boston, New York, 2017.

[29] Martin Wolf, "The U.S. Must Avoid a New Cold War with China", *Financial Times*, October 31, 2018.

[30] Jonathan D. Spence, *To Change China: Western Advisers in China*, 1620-1960, Penguin Books, 1980.

[31] Xi Jinping, Speech at the first China International Import Expo, November 5, 2018.

[32] Martin Jacques, *When China Rules the World: The End of the Western World and Birth of a New Global Order*, Second Edition, Penguin Books, 2012.

[33] Martin Wolf, "The U.S. Must Avoid a New Cold War with China", *Financial Times*, October 31, 2018.

[34] Henry M. Paulson, Jr. , *The United States and China at a Crossroads*, Speech at Asia Society, November 16, 2018.

[35] Martin Jacques, *When China Rules the World: The End of the Western World and Birth of a New Global Order*, Second Edition, Penguin Books, 2012, p. 10.

[36] Kevin Rudd, "How to Avoid An Avoidable War: Ten Questions About the New U.S. China Strategy", *Foreign Affairs*, October 22, 2018.

[37] Kevin Rudd, "How to Avoid An Avoidable War: Ten Questions About the New U.S. China Strategy", *Foreign Affairs*, October 22, 2018.

[38] Martin Wolf, "The U.S. Must Avoid a New cold War with China", *Financial Times*, October 31, 2018.

Chapter Two

Spring and Autumn, Warring States and Chicken Soup for the Soul

"The secret ingredient of my secret ingredient soup is ... nothing."

—Kung Fu Panda (2005), Hollywood

On Oct. 30, 2018, lionized Chinese novelist Jin Yong died at 94. Jin's stories are the apotheosis of a popular genre known in Chinese as *wuxia*, which mainly consists of swashbuckling martial arts adventures. Mourning swept across Chinese cyberspace.

Jin never won a Nobel literature prize that Westerners adore. His death, however, aroused waves of nostalgia in nearly all Chinese media, both serious and entertainment ones. A blaze of publicity followed for days in a row.

Any major political or economic news, even on social issues, is usually bound in this Internet era to spread over the globe in an instant. But interestingly, items about the passing away of this Chinese martial arts novelist, hailed as the most influential one of the 20th century, were absent from Western media coverage.

Most Americans wouldn't be saddened by Jin's death, as his works hardly tugged at their heartstrings. It's nobody's fault, of course, but is surely a matter of regional culture. The adventurous world Jin built was once translated into English, yet the brotherhood and chivalry endorsed in *jianghu*, the community of martial artists, confuse American readers.

Later, *The New Yorker*'s comments shed light on Jin's prestige among Chinese readers. "Of course, there were other *wuxia* writers, and there was kung-fu fiction before Jin Yong. Just as there was folk music before Bob Dylan," the magazine wrote[1]. Bob Dylan became a bridge between two different cultures. Yet this bridge of empathy is not wide enough.

Less than two weeks after the loss of Jin, news that Stan Lee passed away was flashed across the world. Lee's name was not familiar to Chinese readers. When fans compared the 95-year-old Lee to Jin, the cultural barrier was torn down. Now people know both were great creators. As Jin has become synonymous with Hong Kong's rich tradition of *wuxia* cinema, Stan Lee is synonymous with American superhero movies.

Yet the bridge between cultures does not necessarily lead deep into people's hearts. Whereas films based on Marvel Comics became huge box-office successes in China, few audiences take these superheroes seriously as their idols. Similarly, of the 14 novels and novellas and one short story Jin wrote, only three were translated into English and none into any other Western language. Some Western scholar thus concludes that now and forever, Western readers can't find the door to the *wuxia* world that Jin created.

Reference can help link two distinctly different cultures. Nevertheless, many elements in one culture cannot find their correspondence in another. Without references, attempts to understand a different culture on no mature contemplation tend to cause cognitive deviation. For example, Americans, after reading Jin's works, may hold that all Chinese vie to be lords of martial arts, while X-Men movies likely paint to the audience in China a picture of the United States aiming to be world police.

It makes no odds if such cognitive deviation exists merely in cinemas or libraries. Once scholars or policymakers exploit it improperly or even gloat over the so-called earth-shattering discovery, they are in fact exposing themselves to ridicule. Such deviation will either become deadly poisons or repeat funny historical mistakes.

One profound such case is the misreading that some American scholars harbor of China's Warring States period from 475 to 221 B.C.

I. Creating Something from Knowing Nothing

Hollywood in 2012 released the American heroic movie *Battleship*, in which Lieutenant Alex Hopper (Taylor Kitsch), a naval officer, fends off an alien armada with tactics and safeguards the earth against the invasion. As he himself said, he fought the enemy where they weren't, which was a key to his success, as is taught by *The Art of War*, an ancient Chinese military treatise. After all these years, Alex thought, that finally just clicked. However, an eye-popper ensued when Captain Yuri Nagata, a Japanese commanding officer who neared Alex, denied it, saying "That's not what it means."

Nagata was correct. The tactics aren't even close to *The Art of War*. Neither is "crossing the sea under camouflage", "looting a burning house", "decking the tree with false blossoms", "taking the opportunity to pilfer a goat", "making the host and the guest exchange roles" or "removing the firewood from under the pot". All these tactics come from the Chinese essay "Thirty-Six Stratagems."

Then, in what does "Thirty-Six Stratagems" have its roots? The term was first seen in *Book of Qi*, a history of the Chinese dynasty Southern Qi from 479 to 502 A.D., centuries later than the Warring States period. The book wrote, as sarcasm, that Tan Daoji, a high-ranking general of the Liu Song dynasty from 420 to 479 A.D., had "36 stratagems" to fight enemies but, once in danger, chose to beat a hasty retreat. Here "36" doesn't refer to any specific figure but means only "quite a lot".

"Thirty-Six Stratagems" as a published book in different languages has an even shorter history. At first, a handwritten copy of a book entitled *Secret Scripts on Art of War* was found in 1941 at an old bookstall in the northwestern Chinese province of Gansu. The book, without an author or a publication date, mainly discusses common sense in preserving health, and in the appendix lists the 36 stratagems. Until 1961, when China's *Guangming Daily* in its supplements introduced the book, the public for the first time acquainted itself with "Thirty-Six Stratagems". After another 18 years, a publishing house finally printed and published the book. Neither "*Secret Scripts*" on "*Art of War*" nor "Thirty-Six Stratagems" ever appeared in any Chinese book catalog down through the ages.

After being translated into other languages, the book was on the radar screen. Since certain tactics in "Thirty-Six Stratagems" drew inspiration from historical stories or idioms circulating in the Spring and Autumn (770-476 B.C.) and Warring States periods, some Westerners believe the book is a classic in the two periods, the treasure of the pre-Qin period or the cream of *The Art of War.* To top it all off, certain American scholars in recent years have borrowed concepts from "Thirty-Six Stratagems", *The Art of War* and *Strategies of the Warring States* to explain a modern world, accusing China of, by pre-Qin ploys, cheating the world and "crossing the sea under camouflage." Some view it with revulsion that, since China performing half-baked tricks has already shocked other countries, will the world order be completely altered if it goes all out with Warring States tactics?

Such sheer fallacies are worshipped from time to time by best-sellers and think tanks in the West, while for scholars meticulous in ancient Chinese philosophy, they are either yellow journalism that "creates something from nothing" as was mentioned in *The Art of War*, or ignorance that the U.S. academia holds about traditional philosophy in the East. The latter seems more likely. Just as American author Howard Phillips Lovecraft said, "The oldest and strongest kind of fear is fear of the unknown."

II. Borrowlism and Chicken Soup for the Soul

Two civilizations or two cultures, no matter how well one interacts with the other, must in certain aspects be unknown to each other. Among the simplest solutions is Borrowlism, a plain motive of which is for domestic readers to advance their understanding of foreign cultures through storytelling.

Most children in China learn about Western civilizations from textbooks. Many are familiar with a story about Thomas Edison. At the age of 7, Edison arranged mirrors in a way to concentrate candlelight, helping doctors perform his mother's appendicitis surgery. Another fable, in which George Washington admitted to his father that he chopped down a cherry tree with his hatchet and was forgiven, also travels widely. However, intensive discussions about the two stories that were probably manufactured took China by storm on the Internet. People found there was no surgery for appendicitis across the whole world until 1886, some 32 years after Edison reportedly saved his mother's life. Likewise, the cherry-tree myth was invented by a Washington biographer in 1806 to boost his book sales, and in Washington's neighborhood there was no cherry tree. Though kids were taught about the value of ingenuity and honesty by the stories, fake is fake. They will know this one day, just like Lieutenant Alex Hopper in *Battleship* finds there is no such tactic as "fighting the enemy where they weren't" in *The Art of War*.

Museums and documentaries used to be main sources for Westerners to know about China. Once they saw a limit of the sources, they introduced Chinese culture to the West in their own ways. Borrowlism as simple as such caused ironic misapprehensions.

Take *The Art of War* that fascinated Westerners for hundreds of years. Since Western military scientists and sinologists translated the treatise into English, cognitive deviation has snowballed. In 1910 British sinologist Lionel Giles, among pioneers, translated *The Art of War* into English, and in 1963 U.S. military historian Samuel B. Griffith too gave it a try. So far there are more than 40 widely distributed English translations, all in a bid to advise readers by resurrecting Sunzi's thoughts in modern military affairs, business, daily life, or even on golf courses.

The Art of War by Sunzi analyzes aspects of warfare and how they apply to military strategy. To resort to arms or not to, it's a tactic. To fight or not to, it's a choice. War is anything but what Sunzi advocated for. In the treatise, he wrote that war is of vital importance to the state, a matter of life and death, a road either to survival or to ruin, hence, to fight and conquer in all your battles is yet not supreme excellence. Unfortunately, the English title *The Art of War* loses something in translation, for there's neither "war" nor "art" in the Chinese one.

The translation of the title aside, a lot of Western scholars believe that the so-called strategy taught by *The Art of War* was the secret to Qin's conquest of the other states and hence to the end of the Warring States period, based on resulted from which tactics in the treatise were rendered and interpreted one by one, and a riot of road maps to military affairs and business derived from them. Even today, bountiful articles on the Internet remain as an attempt to reveal how the U.S. military works based on *The Art of War*. Western media claimed that Vietnam, since it was familiar with *The Art of War*, defeated the United States in the war; that Tommy Franks, the then-Commander of the U.S.

Central Command, used the tactics during the 2003 invasion of Iraq; and that former Secretary of Defense Donald Henry Rumsfeld was a stalwart of Sunzi. Leave the accuracy of those articles aside for a moment. An inconvenient truth remains that if a book can help anyone be ever victorious, why isn't everyone winning?

Regarding this, Qing dynasty emperor Kangxi (1654-1722) had sense. He once expressed disdain for those who advocated a strict reliance on traditional texts to solve contemporary military problems:

> "For in war it's experience in action that matters. The so-called Seven Military Classics (which include *The Art of War*) are full of nonsense about water and fire, lucky omens and advice on the weather, all at random and contradicting each other. I told my officials once that if you followed these books you would never win a battle ... All one needs is an inflexible will and careful planning"[2]

Kangxi is quite all there. He knew *The Art of War* was not a chicken soup for the soul. Without insights into its philosophical context, a bid to master the treatise will go nowhere. About 17 centuries before Kangxi, *Records of the Grand Historian*, a monumental history of ancient China, had already told a similar story of Zhao Kuo, a general in the Warring States period. Zhao, an armchair strategist, was fond of reading books on military science but remained inexperienced. In resistance against the State of Qin, he got the worst of it and lost his life.

III. History is not a Carnival Mirror

Ecclesiastes said: "What is happening now has happened before, and what will happen in the future has happened before, because God makes the same things happen over and over again." This provides insight akin to an old

Chinese saying, "Consult history when observing reality, and reality does not exist without history." Both, for edification, told later generations to draw lessons from bygone days.

Understanding of history in the East is out of line with the West. As French economist François Quesnay (1694-1774) revealed in his book *Despotism in China*, "With regard to history, it is a part of literature which has been cultivated in China, in all times, with unparalleled ardor; there are few nations who have brought so much care to write their annals, and who preserve more preciously their historical monuments."[3]

In the West, the term "history" originated from the Greek *historia*, meaning "inquiry" or "knowledge acquired by investigation". In 1582 the Gregorian calendar was introduced by Pope Gregory XIII of the Catholic Church and was later widely accepted. Modern historiography with scrupulous methods just began during the Age of Enlightenment, and in the 19th century, historian became a profession. Most of previous history was told by archaeological excavations. For instance, near the ruins of the great walls at Mycenae in Greece, a German-born businessman found a circle of graves at the end of the 19th century. A lost civilization called Mycenaean from approximately 1600 to 1100 B.C. was then unearthed.

In China, it's not the case. There have been annals of Chinese history since the first year of the Gonghe Regency in 841 B.C. From 722 B.C. on, recorded history has been accurate in dates. Throughout the 550-year Spring and Autumn and Warring States period, major events in almost every year were written down in ancient books. China has since then recorded its history year after year, a globally unique phenomenon.

"All history is the history of thought," wrote English historian Robin George Collingwood (1889-1943) in his book *The Idea of History*.[4] "The processes of nature can ... be properly described as sequences of mere events, but those of history cannot. What the historian is looking for is these processes of thought." From this perspective, it doesn't take much imagination to see that China has internalized historical records passed on from one generation to another. Different from contractual interpersonal relationships in the West, Chinese adhere to social connections with morality as the bulk.

The Warring States period, for example, saw the flowering of ancient Chinese philosophy, when an army of great thinkers like Confucius, Mencius, Laozi, Zhuangzi, Mozi and Han Feizi took the stage. Whereas some Chinese today may never read *Spring and Autumn Annals* compiled by Confucius or *Tao Te Ching* written by Laozi, their behaviors reflect morals and ethical codes rooted in the Warring States period. Here the power of history is displayed. In the form of social edification, it civilizes people by osmosis.

Individual Western scholars, with no knowledge of this, tend to feel surprised when they come across one thought in an ancient Chinese book and consider it a solution, as if a groundbreaking discovery to some unsolved mystery of modern China, such as a specific policy in today's China, has its origins in a story or an idiom from some ancient books.

Do you really believe Newton all of a sudden came up with his theory of gravity when an apple fell on his head?

IV. External Moves and Internal Works

Many Chinese Kung fu movies, as well as many Kungfu stars such as Bruce Lee, are very popular in the United States.

The U.S. media discussed why Bruce Lee is so popular. Some like his explosive power while punching the helmet. Some like his protection force while facing a fight. Some like his muscle quality. Some like his side kick that has hundreds of pounds of force. And some like his avant-garde Jeet Kune Do moves.

Bruce Lee's moves and routines are right there. Why is it so hard for another person to surpass him in Jeet Kune Do attainment?

The reason lies in the knowledge behind Bruce Lee's moves.

On Bruce Lee's epitaph, there is a Taiji design and two lines of Chinese characters: "Using no way as way, having no limitation as limitation." This is the core of the Jeet Kune Do moves and the core of Jeet Kune Do philosophy.

The sentence can be interpreted in a variety of ways. In short, it is "the natural, intangible shape of the Tao". Like water in its natural state, it has no shape. If it is poured into a cup, it has the shape of the cup; if it is poured into a bucket, it has the shape of the bucket. If you kick it or hit it, it will splash back; if you hold a handful of water, it will yield; if you press it, it will slip away through your fingers. The softest thing fears strike the least.

The core meaning could be used in boxing, being a human, doing business and governing a country. The philosophical thoughts in it were derived from Taoism during the Spring and Autumn and Warring States period, and later joined the theory of Zen.

This is the relation between external moves and internal works.

The core of the Spring and Autumn period and the Warring States period could be summed up as external moves and internal works. The moves are external performance, which means exchanging blows and the strategy of offense and defense. The internal works are internal cultivation, a galaxy of philosophy and the intersection of minds. The intricate wording of *Sunzi's Art of War* seems like talking about the tactics of using military forces, but in fact, it is about the truth of interaction with others. The obscure phrase of *Tao Te Ching* seems like talking about self-cultivation, governing a country, using military forces and keeping in good health. In fact, it is still a way of interacting with other people. The "vertical alliance" and "horizontal alliance" look like external moves, but the way to convince others to join you and ally with you relies on internal works.

Without internal works, the external moves are doomed to be idle talker and surface acting. If a person provokes disputes one after another, sanctions one to another, and gathers a group to fight against another in the name of something, he may be successful for one time, but he can't make great progress and earn the respect of others.

In the international arena, China has been cultivating its own internal strengths and applying the tradition of virtue-based interactions to international relations. Five principles of peaceful coexistence, good neighborliness, openness and inclusiveness, cooperation and mutual benefit, help the less developed ... All these are the inheritance and interpretation of the essence of the pre-Qin Dynasty ideology.

This is actually the true value of the Spring and Autumn and Warring States period for us now.

V. States Without War

The Chinese have never stopped comprehending the Spring and Autumn and Warring States. Many civilizations in the world have also sought inspirations in the Spring and Autumn and Warring States from centuries ago.

The earliest and most influential ideology school in the Chinese pre-Qin Dynasty is Laozi's *Tao Te Ching*. As early as 1,000 years ago in the Tang Dynasty, the *Tao Te Ching* was spread far away to the Korean Peninsula and India. At the end of the Ming Dynasty, a large number of Western missionaries came to China to preach, opening the real cultural exchanges between Europe and China. *Tao Te Ching* started its journey to the West, and was widely translated and studied beyond China. The masterpiece has been translated into 28 languages and rendered in more than 1,100 versions, ranking first in foreign translating of Chinese books. The English version of the *Tao Te Ching* was widely spread to Europe and the United States at the end of the Qing Dynasty. From 1886 to 1924, there were 16 English versions of the *Tao Te*

Ching, and from the 1920s to the 1960s, there were more than 40 English versions.[5] Moreover, during this period, the translation of *Tao Te Ching* echoed the Chinese translation of *the Bible*, which has a strong social and political influence.[6]

At the end of the 20th century, the Cold War came to an end. The international community moved toward political multi-polarization, economic globalization and cultural diversification. To seek new development for Western civilization, scholars from all academic fields turned to the study of Taosim, trying to find the revelation of the Eastern wisdom in their field. In this period, English versions of *Tao Te Ching* were published at an unprecedented speed. The total number of English versions during this period was 78, of which 59 were published in the United States.[7]

Obviously, the Chinese pre-Qin wisdoms have more or less affected many Americans, including politicians. For example, in 1988, then-U.S. President Ronald Reagan quoted Laozi's view of "Govern a great nation as you would cook a small fish; do not overdo it" in his "State of the Union Address" to explain his opinion on the free market.

In other fields, the pre-Qin ideology was also used by some Americans, including composer John Milton Cage (1912-1992). In a 1952 concert, Cage asked the pianist to sit down in front of the piano and open the piano cover. The audience sat quietly waiting in the light. One minute, no movement; two minutes, no movement; three minutes, people began to get restless, looking around and wondering what was happening. Four minutes and 33 seconds, the pianist closed the piano cover, stood up and said: "Thank you, ladies and gentlemen. I've just finished playing '4 minutes and 33 seconds.'"

Cage's sheet music reads:

4 minutes and 33 seconds

The first movement (I)

TACET

The second movement (II)

TACET

The third movement (III)

TACET

Nobody can really hear the music? Why did the audience feel restless in their hearts?

It was discovered that a year before this silent concert, one of Cage's students gifted him an English version of *The Book of Changes*. Cage realized that the most basic element of music is not to play, but to listen.

The Book of Changes is considered the most profound and incomprehensible book in the pre-Qin classics. It is also regarded as the "source of the Tao" and the "head of the classics" in Chinese literature. It is superficially a book about divinatory symbols, but actually it is a philosophical classic that explains the relations between humans and nature. Confucius especially loved *The Book of Changes* and prefaced it in his later years.

"4 minutes and 33 seconds" also reflects the philosophy of Laozi. "A large square seems cornerless, a great vessel is the last completed, a great sound is inaudible, a great image is formless," Laozi said in the *Tao Te Ching*.

So, is silence being silent?

Taking a broad view of today's international arena, being silent is often an attitude, and sometimes even more powerful than making a voice.

It is a pity that some always think being silent means timidness or even conspiracy.

Rather than using conspiracy theories to read the world, it would be better to take a look at a dialogue in the Hollywood animated movie *Kung Fu Panda*:

"The secret ingredient of my secret ingredient soup is ... nothing."

"To make something special, you just have to believe it's special."

"There is no secret ingredient. It's just you."

[1] Frisch, N. (2018). The Gripping Stories, and Political Allegories, of China's Best-Selling Author, *The New Yorker*. https://www.newyorker.com/books/page-turner/the-gripping-stories-and-political-allegories-of-chinas-best-selling-author (Accessed: 16 November 2018).

[2] Sullivan, J. F. (2018). A New Sunzi Translation: Is There Any Blood Left in This Old Stone? The Strategy Bridge. https://thestrategybridge.org/the-bridge/2018/7/5/reviewing-a-new-sun-tzu-translation-is-there-any-blood-left-in-this-old-stone (Accessed: 16 November 2018).

[3] Quesnay, François. (1992). *Zhonghua diguo de zhuanzhi zhidu [Despotism in China]* (Tan Min, Trans.). Beijing: The Commercial Press. 57.

[4] Collingwood, R. G. (1946). *The Idea of History*. Oxford: Oxford University Press. 215.

[5] Zhao, Y. H.. (2003). *The Muse from Cathay*. Shanghai: Shanghai Translation Publishing House. 314.

[6] Wang, J. F. (2001). Centre and Margin: On the Early English Translations of the Tao-te-ching. *Chung-Wai Literary Monthly*, 30(3), 114-132.

[7] Xin, H. J. & Gao, S. B.. (2008). Diachronic Description of Tao Te Ching in the English World. *Journal of Nanjing Agricultural University (Social Sciences Edition)*, 8(1), 79-84.

Chapter Three

Nixon and Kissinger

In order to survive together in mankind's uncertain future, Americans and Chinese will have to find some common ground in their understanding of their common history, as to how they dealt with each other in times past.

— John King Fairbank, "The United States and China"

I. Secret Letter

On the evening of June 2, 1971, in the heart of Washington, the capital of the United States, the White House, a 200-year-old English country style building, was shining like a piece of white jade in the lights of lamps and the moon.

At the brightly lit Lincoln Hall in the White House, President Richard Nixon was reading and processing documents when his National Security Adviser Henry Kissinger came in. Since Nixon took office, Kissinger had been helping the president manage relations with China.

Kissinger must have been running from the West Wing of the White House to the president because he was out of breath. He handed the president two pages of paper saying, this was just brought by Pakistan with a diplomatic pouch. The letter said:

Premier Zhou Enlai has seriously studied President Nixon's messages of April 29, May 17 and May 22, 1971, and has repeated with much pleasure to Chairman Mao Zedong that President Nixon is prepared to accept his suggestion to visit Beijing for direct conversations with the leaders of the People's Republic of China. Chairman Mao Zedong has indicated that he welcomes President Nixon's visit and looks forward to that occasion when he may have direct conversation with His Excellency the President, in which each side would be free to raise the principle issue of concern to it.

Premier Zhou Enlai welcomes Dr. Kissinger to China as the S. representative who will come in advance for a preliminary secret meeting with high-level Chinese officials to prepare and make necessary arrangements for President Nixon's visit to Beijing.[1]

Nixon had awaited the letter for two weeks.

"This is the most important communication that has come to an American president since the end of World War II,"[2] Kissinger said after Nixon read the letter.

That was the night when Kissinger's world-shaking secret visit to China was confirmed. Nixon and Kissinger were too excited to sleep. Nixon and Kissinger, who rarely drank at night, opened an old Courvoisier brandy and drank just enough wine.

During their talks, they mentioned Marco Polo, an Italian merchant, explorer and writer who travelled to China in the 13th century and described to Europeans the wealth and great size of China.

They also decided on the code name for Kissinger's trip — The Polo Operation — which Kissinger would use if the presidential trip had been arranged.[3]

In Chinese, "letter" is both a physical letter and a message that is exchanged between two sides and endowed with the meaning of trust.

This dramatic event during Nixon's presidency was at the top of the list because the president believed that confidentiality was required for Kissinger's visit to China.

A month later, Kissinger embarked on the secret diplomatic mission. The precursory stops on the trip took him through Saigon, Bangkok, New Delhi and Rawalpindi.

After Kissinger feigned a stomach ache and declined visitors in Rawalpindi, the visiting-China core team including Kissinger and Winston Lord flew over the mountains into China.

On July 9, the U.S. delegation arrived in Beijing and began to observe China, listen to China and talk to China in the next 48 hours.

Kissinger finally met with Zhou Enlai. This was the first time since the founding of the People's Republic of China that senior officials of the two countries shook hands for the first time in more than 20 years.

China and the United States maintained a tacit understanding of mutual trust on Kissinger's secret visit to Beijing. Only when Kissinger quietly flew back to Pakistan, completed his subsequent schedule and returned to the United States did the leaders of both sides make the July 15 Announcement of Kissinger's secret China trip and Nixon's forthcoming one.

The meeting between the leaders of China and the United States was to seek the normalization of relations between the two countries and also to exchange views on questions of concerns to the two countries, according to the document. Behind this brief announcement lay more than two years of complex, subtle, and determined diplomatic signals and negotiations. China and the United States had maintained the almost miraculous secrecy.[4]

The world was shocked.

II. Multiple Channels

Nothing on earth lives without laws. The word "Tao", brought out by the ancient Chinese philosopher and writer Laozi, could signify principles, conventions, methods and ways among its many differing uses. Philosophically, it could refer to the natural order of the universe. In real life, it could be identified as channels.

Such channels secure the interactions between China and the United States.

Before China and the United States established diplomatic relations in 1979, the two sides used three ways for communication: a series of ambassadorial talks from 1955-1970; three back-channels, namely the Pakistani channel and the Romanian channel, the Paris channel, and the UN channel, which played a key role during Nixon's and Kissinger's visits to China; face-to-face dialogues between Chinese and U.S. leaders after Nixon's visit; and direct official interactions through liaison offices.[5]

History testifies that messengers and channels were critical to China-U.S. relations.

Before Beijing and Washington renewed face-to-face high-level meetings, communications relied heavily on oral messages and letters, as ambassadorial meetings between Chinese and U.S. officials in Warsaw had yielded little.

In those days when public contacts between the two countries were so intermittent, high-level officials embraced back-channels in confidence to exchange messages key to future growth of bilateral relations, in which process Pakistan and Romania became leading messengers.[6]

On October 25, 1970, Pakistani President Agha Muhammad Yahya Khan met Nixon in Washington, and the U.S. president grasped this opportunity to build the Yahya channel so Washington could send messages to Beijing via Pakistan.

Nixon used the occasion of his Asian and European trip in 1969 to tell the

Pakistani and Romanian presidents that he sought high-level exchanges with Chinese leaders. In his toast at the welcoming banquet in Romania, Nixon for the first time intentionally referred to Communist China by its official name, the People's Republic of China (PRC), sending out a significant signal to the world.

On October 25, 1970, Romanian President Nicolae Ceausescu started his state visit to the United States. During a meeting between the two leaders, Nixon told his Romanian counterpart that Washington fully welcomed exchanges of high-level personal representatives between the United States and China, even short of the ultimate ideal of reestablishing full diplomatic relations. Ceausescu promised to deliver the secret message to Beijing, marking the beginning of the "Romanian channel."[7]

U.S. writer and journalist Edgar Snow was another intermediary apart from heads of state of other countries. In October 1970 he was invited by Chairman Mao to tour the top of the rostrum at Tiananmen Square, after which they held a long talk. To Kissinger, Snow's report of this China visit sent out a message that Beijing wanted "to encourage a new phase in the relationship between China and the United States and the world by conveying an altered governance."[8]

China and the United States kept exchanging oral messages and signals for more than two years, until Nixon took the risk to suggest that Kissinger undertake a secret trip to China. Nixon believed that this major proposal was the only way at the critical moment to save the two countries from slipping back into another long round of tentative probing. "I decided that the time had come to take the big step and propose a presidential visit," Nixon wrote.[9]

After Kissinger's secret visit to China in July 1971, the two countries agreed to build another channel within the control of the two leaders and without the help of a third country.[10]

It was the Paris channel, a way that made a great contribution to fixing China-U.S. relations.

The Paris channel saw U.S. military attache in France Vernon A. Walters and Chinese ambassador in Paris Huang Zhen as the two representatives, while Kissinger, the national security adviser under Nixon, was the man in charge on the U.S. side.

Kissinger said he would deliver unsigned documents to China through the Paris channel, and he would personally reach Huang Zhen in Paris if anything important happened. This was how Paris became the secret liaison for exchanging messages for China and the United States.[11] It did much preparation work for Nixon's China visit in 1972.

And the tempo started to speed up considerably.

III. Dancing Together

China and the United States began contact with each other after a 20-year standstill. The values of the two sides are very different, and it can even be said to be the opposite. To break the deadlock in the two countries' relations, it is impossible to rely on one side alone.

Under the dark clouds of the Cold War, China and the United States, deeply involved in the Korean War, have been in the state of hostility for quite a long time.

Despite that, the two sides had been keeping low-level intergovernmental talks. In June 1954 the two countries held consular-level talks in Geneva, Switzerland, over the issue of returning personnel. In August 1955, the first ambassador-level talks between China and the United States were held in Geneva. By 1970, ambassador-level talks between the two countries had been carried out 136 times.

During the first meeting with Kissinger, Zhou Enlai mentioned the ambassador-level talks. With a trace of disappointment, he said, "There's still no result."[12] However, it was still an important attempt by China and the United States to seek to ease relations with each other.

At that time, without a doubt, it would be awkward for the two countries' diplomats to meet. They had always avoided each other on public occasions. To change the situation, someone needed to take the first step.

It was Walter Stoessel, then U.S. ambassador to Poland, who broke the deadlock. This has also become an evocative and dramatic scene in the diplomatic history between China and the United States.

On the evening of December 3, 1969, the Yugoslav embassy in Warsaw held a fashion show in the Polish capital. Diplomatic envoys from various countries, including the Chinese, attended the event. Ordered by the White House, Stoessel, accompanied by Thomas W. Simons, a liaison from the U.S. side, approached Chinese diplomats and tried to say hello to them, hoping to send a message that the United States was willing to improve ties with China. However, the Chinese diplomats, without instructions, fled the scene and kept distance with their U.S. counterparts.

Then, the two Americans started running after the Chinese, shouting in Polish (the only mutually intelligible language available): "We are from the American embassy. We want to meet your ambassador ... President Nixon said he wanted to resume his talk with the Chinese." Two weeks later, the Chinese ambassador in Warsaw invited Stoessel to a meeting at the Chinese Embassy, to prepare for a resumption of the Warsaw talks.[13]

As Kissinger recalled, at the beginning, each side bent over backward to avoid being perceived as having made the first public move. "The result was a minuet so intricate that both sides could always claim that they were not in contact, so stylized that neither country needed to bear the onus of an initiative that might be rejected, and so elliptical that existing political relations could be continued without the need for consultation on a script that had yet to be written." Between November 1969 and February 1970, there were at least 10 occasions when U.S. and Chinese diplomats in various capitals around the world exchanged words — a remarkable event for both sides.[14]

Before the minuet, there was a silent dance — a fantastic interaction between China and the United States after Nixon came to power.

The Sino-Soviet border conflict, or the Zhenbao Island Incident that occurred in March 1969, inflamed tensions between China and the Soviet Union and brought the two countries to the brink of war. The United States kept a close eye on the Sino-Soviet strained ties. William Rogers, then U.S. secretary of state, several times called for the resumption of China-U.S. talks, saying the United States would not change its basic policy toward China and China's Communist Party, but would change the relations with China. He said even if Washington needed to take unilateral measures at some certain moments, it would make efforts.[15]

In July, Nixon was about to begin his trip to six Asian countries and Romania. Besides the visits, he had an important task — to find a new channel to open the door for U.S.-China ties.

A report from the Associated Press almost disclosed the secret. It said that when it came to Nixon's world trip, an anonymous U.S. official gave an expectation that the tour might open a way for new contacts between America and China. Fortunately, his words did not draw global attention.[16]

Before Nixon's trip was made public, two Americans were held by China as their yacht strayed into China's territorial water off Guangdong. The United States, at the same time, was about to announce measures over easing restrictions on U.S. citizens traveling to mainland China, an effort by the Nixon administration to help build up contacts with Beijing. Therefore, Kissinger decided to postpone the announcement to wait and see whether the Chinese people would use the case to spark a wave of anti-Americanism.

Several days passed, and Beijing remained silent on the issue. On July 21, the U.S. State Department, with a low profile, declared the measures. Two days later, the issue was resolved when Premier Zhou received reports from Guangdong and ordered the immediate release of the two Americans.[17]

No open dialogue, both being low profile — this time, China and the United States used their actions to test each other's attitudes and sincerity.

Ping-pong diplomacy, the exchange of table tennis (ping-pong) players between the United States and China in April 1971, was a stunning "dressage" in the process of resuming exchanges.

On April 6, as Nixon recalled, there was a breakthrough that nobody expected before — the U.S. embassy in Tokyo reported that its table tennis team, in Japan for the 31st World Table Tennis Championships, received an invitation to visit China and play several exhibition games with the Chinese team. "I was as surprised as I was pleased," Nixon later wrote in his memoirs. "I had never expected that the China initiative would come to fruition in the form of a ping-pong team."[18]

The invitation from China became big news in the world.

On April 14, 1971, the young American players met Zhou Enlai at the Great Hall of the People and they were very excited. Most foreign ambassadors to China had never had such a privilege.

"You open a new chapter in the bilateral relations between the Chinese and American peoples. I believe that the new beginning of our friendship will, for sure, gain support from the majorities of both people," Zhou told the U.S. team. The athletes were shocked to hear that they were pushed into the high-level diplomatic track. "Isn't it?" Zhou said, breaking the silence. His words prompted a round of applause.[19]

Although China and the United States had not yet established diplomatic ties, the two countries' dexterous dance steps in the ping-pong diplomacy touched people's hearts and opened the door for friendly exchanges between the two peoples, making Sino-U.S. non-governmental contacts more harmonious and beautiful.

IV. Following Trends

Thanks to the wise judgment by Chinese and U.S. leaders on global trends, the two countries witnessed a change from a dead set to a renewal of communication, from a tentative probing to a sound bilateral relationship.

In the late 1950s, U.S. society observed a strong current of thoughts urging the country to change its tough policy against China. Particularly, such ideas could be found in a report titled "United States Foreign Policy: Asia" by Colon Associates, Ltd, which was also known as the Conlon Asia policy report.[20] However, it was only after Nixon took office that the United States began to seriously consider thawing U.S.-China relations.

Nixon was still anti-communist when the then-President Dwight David Eisenhower held power. Yet, when Nixon took office in 1969, he did a complete 180-degree turn, proposing inviting China back into the world community and expressing a strong wish for friendship with China.

Nixon said in his memoirs that, through an article titled "Asia After Vietnam" published in the October 1967 issue of *Foreign Affairs*, he first brought out the idea that the United States should establish relations with Communist China.

"Taking the long view, we simply cannot afford to leave China forever outside the family of nations, there to nurture its fantasies, cherish its hates and threaten its neighbors. There is no place on this small planet for a billion of its potentially most able people to live in angry isolation," he wrote.[21]

Nixon referred indirectly to the idea again in his inaugural address in January 1969. Less than two weeks later, on February 1, he wrote a memorandum to Kissinger urging that they give every encouragement to the attitude that the administration was exploring possibilities of rapprochement with the Chinese.[22]

Kissinger then started special research on the feasibility of U.S. policy change and concrete steps to take. The research, done by July 1969, suggested that the United States take unilateral measures to warm U.S.-China relations. It was later included in the National Security Study Memorandum (NSSM) and the National Security Division Memorandum (NSDM).[23]

The Sino-Soviet Alliance, built in the 1950s, reflected the unique relations between China and Russia for strategic cooperation and common ideology. With substantial strategic and ideological differences, the alliance finally broke, and bilateral relations deteriorated rapidly. The relationship then dropped to a freezing point after the Zhenbao Island Incident in March 1969, which was also known as the Sino-Soviet border conflict.

The Nixon government recognized this incident and the side benefits of the Vietnam War as an icebreaker of the awkward U.S.-China relations, and Washington started to make a change.

At a National Security Council meeting in August 1969, Nixon chose an attitude. He put forward a shocking thesis that, in the existing circumstances, the Soviet Union was the more dangerous party to the United States and that it would be against U.S. interests if China were "smashed" in a China-Soviet war. To Nixon, on the issue of China, geopolitics trumped other considerations. "It was a revolutionary moment in U.S. foreign policy: an American President declared that we had a strategic interest in the survival of a major Communist country with which we had had no meaningful contact for 20 years and against which we had fought a war and engaged in two military confrontations," Kissinger wrote.[24]

Almost at the same time, Chinese leaders also determined that U.S.-Soviet conflict was the priority, followed by China-Soviet conflict, then by China-U.S.

conflict, and Beijing began its policy change on the United States.

In the article "The Prelude to the Opening of Sino-American Relations," Chinese veteran diplomat Xiong Xianghui said, "It was Chairman Mao's big decision that China opened up its relations with the United States. The decision, which had a far-reaching influence, was made with twists and turns. Its prelude began with Mao assigning four marshals of the Chinese People's Liberation Army to study and discuss current international affairs in late spring 1969."[25]

On July 1, 1969, those four marshals — Chen Yi, Ye Jianying, Xu Xiangqian and Nie Rongzhen, war veterans who had helped found the PRC — handed in a signed report, "A Preliminary Analysis on the Tense International Situation," to Premier Zhou.

"The conflict now lies in the struggles among the three major players in the world — China, the Soviet Union and the United States. It is different from the struggles among seven major players before World War II, and from the U.S.-Soviet frictions right after the war," the analysis said.

"It is unlikely in the near future for the United States and the Soviet Union to invade China separately or together. As the Soviet Union takes us as its major enemy, it is more dangerous than the United States."[26]

The quartet's analysis made a correct judgment on global trends, drew a clear picture of international strategy patterns, and also provided a ground for Chinese leaders to open up China to the United States. Chen Yi, vice premier as well as foreign minister since 1958, later put forward his thoughts on China-U.S. relations that "China should play the American card to make a strategic use of the U.S.-Soviet conflict as well as to advance China-U.S. relations."[27]

History proves that these four marshals who had been suspended from their government and military duties during the Cultural Revolution, especially

Chen Yi who put forward his unconventional thoughts to the government in 1969 amid a tough diplomatic situation, opened the door to the normalization of China-U.S. relations.

The first serious public step in the China initiative was taken in February 1970 when Nixon sent the first Foreign Policy Report to Congress. The section on China started like this:

"The Chinese are a great and vital people who should not remain isolated from the international community ... it is certainly in our interest, and in the interest of peace and stability in Asia and the world, that we take what steps we can toward improved practical relations with Peking."[28]

It was written in the old military treatise by Sunzi, *The Art of War*, that "the onset of troops is like the rush of a torrent which will even roll stones along in its course."

Global trends, like the rush of a torrent, pushed forward some of the great events in China-U.S. diplomatic history. A series of big moves by Chinese and U.S. leaders, extremely in sync and seemingly coincidental, revealed the leaders' abilities to grasp historic opportunities amid global trends.

In March 1970, the U.S. State Department announced a relaxation of most of the official restrictions against travel to Communist China. On April 14, it announced the termination of the 20-year-old embargo on trade between the two sides. Besides, Nixon ordered a series of new steps taken for easing currency and shipping controls applying to China.

The same day, Chinese Premier Zhou Enlai welcomed U.S. table tennis players in Beijing.

On July 15, 1970, China and the United States both announced to the world Nixon's upcoming trip to China at the invitation of Chinese leaders.

The same month, China released U.S. Roman Catholic Bishop James Edward Walsh, who had been arrested in 1958 and held as a prisoner for 12 years.

Early in October, when Nixon gave an interview to "Time" magazine, he said, "If there is anything I want to do before I die, it is to go to China. If I don't, I want my children to."

The same month, Kissinger returned to China for Polo II, or the second Polo Operation. Its purpose was to prepare the agenda for the meetings Nixon would have with Chinese leaders and work out the basic language of the communique that would be issued at the end of Nixon's China visit.

......

"Within a year, Sino-American diplomacy had moved from irreconcilable conflict to a visit to Beijing by a presidential emissary to prepare a visit by the President himself. It did so by sidestepping the rhetoric of two decades and staying focused on the fundamental strategic objective of a geopolitical dialogue leading to a recasting of the Cold War international order," Kissinger wrote.[29]

"That China and the United States would find a way to come together was inevitable given the necessities of the time. It would have happened sooner or later whatever the leadership in either country. That it took place with such decisiveness and proceeded with so few detours is a tribute to the leadership that brought it about. Leaders cannot create the context in which they operate. Their distinctive contribution consists in operating at the limit of what the given situation permits. If they exceed these limits, they crash; if they fall short of what is necessary, their policies stagnate. If they build soundly, they may create a new set of relationships that sustains itself over a historical period because all parties consider it in their own interest," he wrote.[30]

In February 1972, Nixon flew across the Pacific Ocean and arrived in China at last, becoming the first U.S. president to visit the PRC. The whole international community fixed its eyes upon "the week that changed the world."

During his meeting with Zhou Enlai, Nixon admitted broadcasting policies against Chinese objectives once with his U.S. fellows. However, the world had changed, he said, and Washington should adapt to the change to meet U.S. interests.

"My views, because I was in the Eisenhower Administration, were similar to those of Mr. Dulles at that time. But the world has changed since then, and the relationship between the People's Republic and the United States must change too. As the Prime Minister has said in a meeting with Dr. Kissinger, the helmsman must ride with the waves or he will be submerged with the tide," Nixon said.[31]

V. Harmony and Cooperation

Nixon's visit is one of the few occasions where a state visit has brought about a seminal change in international affairs. The reentry of China into the global diplomatic game, and the increased strategic options for the United States, gave a new vitality and flexibility to the international system. Would the interests of the two sides ever be truly congruent? Could they ever separate them from prevalent ideologies sufficiently to avoid tumults of conflicting emotions?[32]

Kissinger's questions can be used to observe the ups and downs of the China-U.S. relations.

As the guiding principles and foundation of the China-U.S. relations, the three joint communiques are the vivid examples of Beijing's and Washington's efforts to seek common ground while reserving differences, get closer to each other and foster win-win cooperation.

The Shanghai Communique released before the resumption of diplomatic ties can be best described as the Confucian philosophy: Harmonious, but different. Just as Nixon said, "What we have said in that communique is not nearly as important as what we will do in the years ahead to build a bridge across 16,000 miles and 22 years of hostility which have divided us in the past."

Though China and the United States have many divergences, principle and pragmatism exist in ambiguous equilibrium in the Shanghai Communique.[33] In particular, both sides reached an agreement on the Taiwan question.

"The U.S. side declared: The United States acknowledges that all Chinese on either side of the Taiwan Strait maintain there is but one China and that Taiwan is a part of China. The United States Government does not challenge that position. It reaffirms its interest in a peaceful settlement of the Taiwan question by the Chinese themselves. With this prospect in mind, it affirms the ultimate objective of the withdrawal of all U.S. forces and military installations from Taiwan. In the meantime, it will progressively reduce its forces and military installations on Taiwan as the tension in the area diminishes."[34]

Kissinger said the most significant of these convergences in the communique was the article on hegemony.

It read: "Neither (side) should seek hegemony in the Asia-Pacific region and each is opposed to efforts by any other country or group of countries to establish such hegemony."[35]

Kissinger noted that the normalization of U.S.-China relations "emerged as a first step toward a common global policy."

U.S. sinologist John King Fairbank said that, after two decades of hostility, the two countries now felt they had more problems in common than there were dividing them.[36]

Fairbank, also a China expert, noted that Nixon's icebreaking trip to Beijing in 1972 launched the normalization process of bilateral relations. In May 1973, China and the United States established liaison offices in each other's capital, which played a significant role in pooling support for the normalization of diplomatic ties, promoting mutual understanding and seeking common ground while reserving differences of the two countries.

However, the pace of normalization fell far short of what Beijing and Washington had anticipated, as it took seven years from Nixon's visit to China in 1972 to the normalization in 1979. Both sides *were partially* responsible for such a long and difficult process.

For the U.S side, Nixon had promised to resume diplomatic ties in his second term. But the Watergate crisis forced Nixon's resignation and brought a lot of difficulties for the Republicans. Gerald Ford, who assumed the presidency after Nixon, tried to avoid making any controversial moves in international affairs.

In China, the Cultural Revolution was continuing and the health of Chairman Mao and Premier Zhou was deteriorating.[37] As Mao grew increasingly frail, the Chinese leadership was locked in a power struggle and a debate over China's destiny, profoundly affecting Sino-U.S. relations.[38]

After Jimmy Carter took office, disagreement arose about which was more important: softening relations with the Soviet Union or normalizing ties with China. One faction, with Secretary of State Cyrus Vance as its representative, proposed that U.S.-China relations should serve the interests of ties with the Soviet Union. The other faction, with National Security Adviser Zbigniew Brzezinski as its leader, proposed that formalizing ties with China should top the government's agenda.

Carter, whose birthday happens to fall on October 1, the National Day of the People's Republic of China, associates with China in many aspects.

As it turned out, Carter and his top advisers reaffirmed the basic principles of the relationship, including those with respect to Taiwan personally affirmed by Nixon during his visit to Beijing. At the same time, the advent of Deng Xiaoping and the collapse of the Gang of Four gave the dialogue between

China and the United States a new pragmatic dimension.[39]

On Nov. 29, 1978, Deng met the Japanese delegation led by Komei Party Chairman Yoshikatsu Takeiri in Beijing and expressed his willingness to establish diplomatic ties with the United States as soon as possible.

"It's my longtime wish to visit Japan. But I also hope to visit Washington. Once China and the U.S. normalize their relations, I will visit the U.S. if Chairman Hua Guofeng couldn't make it. Then I can go to see Marx."

Takeiri asked how long would it take to establish ties with the United States.

Deng said frankly: "It all depends on President Carter's decision. It takes one second to finalize the China-Japan Treaty of Peace and Friendship and it will double the effort, which is two seconds, to normalize China-U.S. relations."[40]

On Dec. 16, 1978, China and the United States issued a joint communique, announcing the establishment of diplomatic relations between the two sides as of Jan. 1, 1979.

On Jan. 1, 1979, China and the United States established diplomatic relations at the ambassadorial level, and on the same day, Washington announced the rupture of official ties with Taiwan. The United States withdrew all its troops stationed in Taiwan before the end of the year and abrogated the Mutual Defense Treaty signed with Taiwan.

Thus China and the United States ended three decades of hostility and their relationship entered into a new historical phase.

The news shocked the whole world. Though there was the unresolved Taiwan question and the United States didn't plan to completely abandon its willingness to interfere in China's internal affairs at that time, the establishment of diplomatic ties represented a momentous turning point in the two countries' relationship, and Sino-U.S. relations ushered in a new era.

Chas Freeman, a veteran diplomat who served as Nixon's interpreter when the then-U.S. president visited China in 1972, said, "From the lengthy and difficult process by which the United States and China moved from mutual hostility through cautious detente to rapprochement represents more than the mere normalization of political relations. In advancing relations to a new stage beyond detente — to a close consultative relationship based on equality, enlightened self-interest, and mutual respect for the different ideologies and social systems of the two countries ..."[41]

However, Deng Xiaoping saw the world.

On Jan. 29, 1979, Deng met with Carter in the White House for the first time. Deng said during his whirlwind tour of the United States that the meaning of the normalization of relations went far beyond the two countries. To maintain a friendly and cooperative relationship between China and the United States is not only in the basic interests of the two peoples, but also conducive to peace and development of the Pacific Ocean and the world.

Deng noted that the two sides bear unshakable responsibilities to make joint efforts to contribute to safeguarding world peace, security and stability, which is an overriding concern for the world.

The China-U.S. relationship was at a new starting point and the world situation was also experiencing a new turn, Deng said.

China and the United States are both great countries with great peoples, and a friendly relationship between the two countries will surely exert far-reaching influence on the international situation, he added.[42]

The China-U.S. relationship has undergone a series of difficult moments in the past few decades, such as the Taiwan Relations Act, 1989 political turbulence in Beijing, the Taiwan Strait Crisis, the NATO bombing of the Chinese embassy in the former Federal Republic of Yugoslavia, and the battle plane crash incident between China and the United States, among others. Freeman used a vivid metaphor to explain the Sino-U.S. relationship which is full of twists and turns: When you have a complicated relationship with a certain person who has a different gender, background and opinions from you, you'll fight sometimes even if you love each other. If you have enough common sense to understand, you don't have to fight all the time. You can solve the problem and move on.

On Dec. 10, 1989, Deng met in Beijing with Brent Scowcroft and Lawrence Sidney Eagleburger, special envoys of U.S. President George H.W. Bush. Deng said although there are some disputes and big differences between China and the United States, the two countries' relations should eventually be improved.

"This is the need of world peace and stability," Deng noted.

What would the world be like if China and the United States didn't have a successful negotiation on the normalization? After decades, Carter still believed that the world would be totally different and much worse than it is now.

The world needs a harmonious coexistence of China and the United States.

VI. Changing World

"In the two centuries since Sino-American contact began in 1784, the Chinese universe has moved from the distant trans-Pacific horizon onto our doorstep. It is more vast and diverse than ever, developing rapidly and unpredictably." That's how Fairbank felt in the 1980s.

Fairbank said in Sino-American relations to 1949, China was always the weaker party, in trouble, the recipient of American interest and philanthropy. America was always the superior party, not in such trouble, able to help. It was not an equal relationship, which is no doubt why Washington enjoyed it.

In 1972 President Nixon's spectacular trip to China began still another cycle of ultra-enthusiasm tapering off into mixed feelings. Now our problem is dual: to accept China's irreducible differentness and yet treat China as a mature and independent equal.[43]

When China and the United States first restored relations 40 years ago, the most significant contribution of the leaders of the time was their willingness to raise their sights beyond the immediate issues of the day.[44] History has taught us that whenever the China-U.S. relationship gets weak and sensitive, our leaders could always look at the big picture and steer the relationship in the right direction with their strategic visions.

Sino-U.S. relations have made steady progress despite ups and downs over the past 40 years. Given the various challenges and profound changes in the world landscape, bilateral relations have been adjusted several times so as to fit the new circumstances, maintain strategic stability and achieve win-win cooperation.

Entering the 21st century, Sino-American ties are getting closer and exchanges between the two sides are expanding at all levels and in different fields, while facing some new uncertainties and challenges.

"Who doesn't want a good China-U.S relationship? Most people want a good one. Because China is the world's biggest developing country and the United States is the biggest developed country, there is no reason to be unfriendly to each other," said Former Foreign Minister Li Zhaoxing in his memoirs.[45]

Think globally, there is no other bilateral relationship that could achieve great progress after undergoing such a bumpy road and share numerous common interests while facing so many divergences. In this rapidly changing society, Sino-American relations at the crossroads of history are faced with new challenges that are incomparable with those of 40 years ago.

The direction of the course of history is not decided by a certain period of time, but by the accumulation of thousands of occurrences of events and dealings with problems. Only after the trend of the world has already formed can people observe the panorama of changes. In this process, the performances and the choices of China, the United States and other countries around the globe will have a great impact on the direction of the world.

Kissinger, the 95-year-old diplomat and renowned strategist, visited Beijing in November 2018. He said cooperation between the United States and China is essential for peace and prosperity in the world, adding that developing U.S.-China relations demands strategic thinking and foresight.

Relations between big countries serve as the cornerstone for the world's stability. China-U.S. ties are of global importance. The start of Sino-American relations is out of strategic considerations, not emotional reasons. The decades of interactions between China and the United States have not only benefited both peoples, but other regions as well, and have become a driving force in global development.

At present, the world is undergoing profound changes and the international community expects China-U.S. relations to develop on the right course. Both sides are faced with a common issue: can China and the United States join hands to build a stable and new international order?

Cooperation leads to win-win results while conflict ends up with a loss for both sides or a disaster for the world. The key to making a right decision for the two countries lies in an accurate judgment of each other's strategic intentions, not jumping into the "Thucydides's trap" with closed eyes.

History tells us that a relationship that features mutual respect, equal consultation and win-win cooperation is the only right choice for the two countries. Only by following the trend of times, deepening their mutual understanding, strengthening their strategic communication and cooperation, properly managing their differences and exploring the right way to get along under the new circumstances can the China-U.S. relationship achieve greater development in the next 40 years.

For the happiness and benefit of the two peoples and the world, the United States and China both need to "coevolve", cultivate friendly feelings and increase strategic mutual trust in this integrated world so as to push through the construction of a cooperation-based international order.

Just like Chas Freeman said, if our interactions were given a broader view, they could promote our world to a much better direction. "We owe it to ourselves and to our posterity to try harder to work together to advance the many strategic interests we have in common."

[1] Richard Nixon, *RN: The Memoirs of Richard Nixon*, New York: Simon & Schuster, 1990, pp.551-552.
[2] Ibid., p.552.
[3] Chen Dunde, *The Week That Changed the World — Documentary of the Handshake Between Mao Tse-Tung and Nixon*, Beijing: China Youth Publishing Group, 2014, pp.314-356.
[4] Richard Nixon, *RN: The Memoirs of Richard Nixon*, New York: Simon & Schuster, 1990, pp.544-545.
[5] Yang Jiemian, "The Changing Patterns of China-US Diplomatic Interactions," *The Chinese Journal of American Studies*, No. 4, 2018.
[6] Ibid.
[7] Richard Nixon, *RN: The Memoirs of Richard Nixon*, New York: Simon & Schuster, 1990, p.546.
[8] Henry Kissinger, *On China*, New York: The Penguin Press, 2011, p.227.
[9] Richard Nixon, *RN: The Memoirs of Richard Nixon*, New York: Simon & Schuster, 1990, pp.550-551.
[10] Ibid., pp.549-550.
[11] Cao Guisheng, "Recalling the 'Secret Paris Channel' between China and the United States", *World Affairs*, No. 18, 1996.
[12] "Memorandum of Conversation," U.S. Department of State, *Foreign Relations of the United States (FRUS)*, 1969-1976, Vol. XVII, (CHINA 1969-1972), p.365.
[13] Henry Kissinger, *On China*, New York: The Penguin Press, 2011, p.221.
[14] Henry Kissinger, *On China*, New York: The Penguin Press, 2011, p.220.
[15] Chen Dunde, *The Week That Changed the World — Documentary of the Handshake Between Mao Tse-Tung and Nixon*, Beijing: China Youth Publishing Group, 2014, pp.129-162.

[16] Ibid.
[17] Chen Dunde, *The Week That Changed the World — Documentary of the Handshake Between Mao Tse-Tung and Nixon*, Beijing: China Youth Publishing Group, 2014, pp.129-162.
[18] Richard Nixon, *RN: The Memoirs of Richard Nixon*, New York: Simon & Schuster, 1990, p.548.
[19] Henry Kissinger, *On China*, New York: The Penguin Press, 2011, p.232.
[20] Tao Wenzhao, *The History of Sino-US Relations (1949-1972)*, Shanghai: Shanghai People's Publishing House, 2004, p.491.
[21] Richard Nixon, "Asia After Vietnam," *Foreign Affairs*, October 1967 Issue.
[22] Richard Nixon, *RN: The Memoirs of Richard Nixon*, New York: Simon & Schuster, 1990, p.545.
[23] Chen Dunde, *The Week That Changed the World — Documentary of the Handshake Between Mao Tse-Tung and Nixon*, Beijing: China Youth Publishing Group, 2014, pp.245-277.
[24] Henry Kissinger, *On China*, New York: The Penguin Press, 2011, p.218.
[25] Xiong Xianghui, "The Prelude to the Opening of Sino-American Relations," *History Materials of the Communist Party of China*, Vol. 42, June 1992.
[26] Ibid.
[27] Xiong Xianghui, "The Prelude to the Opening of Sino-American Relations," *History Materials of the Communist Party of China*, Vol. 42, June 1992.
[28] Richard Nixon, *RN: The Memoirs of Richard Nixon*, (New York: Simon & Schuster), 1990, p.545.
[29] Henry Kissinger, *On China*, New York: The Penguin Press, 2011, p.234.
[30] Henry Kissinger, *On China*, New York: The Penguin Press, 2011, p.215.
[31] "Memorandum of Conversation: Beijing, February 21, 1972, 5:58–6:55 p.m.," *Foreign Relations of the United States (FRUS)*, 1969-1976, Vol. XVII, (CHINA 1969-1972), p.689.
[32] Henry Kissinger, *On China*, New York: The Penguin Press, 2011, p.274.
[33] Henry Kissinger, *On China*, New York: The Penguin Press, 2011, p.271.
[34] "Joint Statement Following Discussion with Leaders of the People's Republic of China: Shanghai, February 22, 1972," *Foreign Relations of the United States (FRUS)*, 1969-1976, Vol. XVII, (CHINA 1969-1972), pp.814-815.
[35] Ibid., p.814.
[36] John King Fairbank, *The United States and China: Fourth Edition, Enlarged*, Cambridge, USA: Harvard University Press, 1983, p.458.
[37] Tao Wenzhao, *A Hundred Years of China-U.S. Relations*, China Social Sciences Press, 2001, p.38.
[38] Henry Kissinger, *On China*, New York: The Penguin Press, 2011, p.297.
[39] Henry Kissinger, *On China*, New York: The Penguin Press, 2011, p.378.
[40] Chen Dunde, *China-US Diplomatic Relationship Establishment — Documentary*

of the Handshake Between DENG Xiaoping and Carter, Beijing: China Youth Publishing Group, 2014, pp.519-543.

[41] Chas W. Freeman, Jr., *Interesting Times: China, America, and the Shifting Balance of Prestige*, Charlottesville, USA: Just World Books, 2012, p.78.

[42] Chen Dunde, *China-US Diplomatic Relationship Establishment — Documentary of the Handshake Between DENG Xiaoping and Carter*, Beijing: China Youth Publishing Group, 2014, pp.589-620.

[43] John King Fairbank, *The United States and China: Fourth Edition, Enlarged*, Cambridge, USA: Harvard University Press, 1983, p.320.

[44] Henry Kissinger, *On China*, New York: The Penguin Press, 2011, p.529.

[45] Li Zhaoxing, *Untold Diplomacy*, Beijing: China CITIC Press, 2014, p.3.

Chapter Four

Self Changing and the Myth to Change China

"The only thing we have to fear is fear itself."

— Franklin D. Roosevelt

"One thing I wished most was to make it possible for the villagers to have meat and have it often," Chinese President Xi Jinping said at a welcoming dinner in Seattle during his first state visit to the United States starting from Sept. 22, 2015. He was recalling his experience as a teenage peasant in the small village of Liangjiahe in Yan'an, Shaanxi Province in the 1960s.[1] At that time, the juvenile Xi and the villagers lived in "earth caves" and slept on "earth beds". Life there was so difficult that people could hardly have meat in their diet for months. After more than 50 years, the teenager has become the leader of China.

At the Spring Festival of 2015, President Xi returned to the village of Liangjiahe, and found that blacktop roads stretched through the village and villagers there were living in brick-and-tile houses with Internet access.

Elderly folks there were covered by basic old-age care and all villagers received medical care coverage. Children were in school. And of course, meat was readily available. Among the hundreds of thousands of villages in China, Liangjiahe is just a microcosm of the dramatic reform in the country. In October 2017, the U.S. Discovery Channel launched a three-episode documentary titled *China: Time of Xi*, which used Xi's experience in Liangjiahe to illustrate the Communist leader's "people-centered" political ideas. Xi once said, "To anyone charged with the governance of China, their primary mission is to focus all the resources on improving people's living standard and gradually achieve common prosperity."

From a poor country where the people did not have enough food to eat, let alone meat, to one of the middle- and high-income countries, Chinese people have been continuing to conduct self-reform, explore a path of socialist modernization with Chinese characteristics and build an effective governance system that is in line with China's national conditions. Meanwhile, those external forces that try to reshape China often fall into misunderstandings about China, resulting in unrealistic fantasies and illusory fears.

I. Exploring the Chinese Path to Democracy

It has been the unremitting pursuit of the Chinese people in the past 170-plus years to live and work in peace and happiness, and to make the country strong and prosperous. After the Opium War in 1840, China fell into a semicolonial and semifeudal society, and Chinese people were called "sick man of East Asia" by foreigners. Since then, countless benevolent Chinese people have struggled in seeking a path to save the nation from doom, from learning the advanced technology of the West to spreading Western culture and ideas, and to introducing the Western constitutional system to China via revolution. Various kinds of reform and restoration schemes were staged in turn.

The outbreak of the May 4th Movement in 1919 was an epoch-making event, which brought the concepts of "democracy" and "science" to China. Chinese intellectuals at that time personalized the two concepts and named them "Mr. De" and "Mr. Sai" in Chinese, based on English pronunciation. Since then, the ideas of democracy and scientific rationality have become an important guide for many people trying to explore China's future way. Chen Duxiu, one of the important founders of the Communist Party of China (CPC), said that only these two Misters can save China out of the political, moral, academic and ideological darkness at that time.

However, it was not a smooth road for the Chinese people to pursue democracy. When "Mr. De" first came to China, many Chinese people's understanding of democracy remained on just shallow levels such as formations of the political organizations and activity procedures in the Western countries.

The Republic of China, established after the 1911 revolution, not only called itself a republican regime, but also adopted the Western parliamentary, multiparty-ruling system and universal suffrage in China. However, grafting democracy this way didn't go along with China's national conditions at that time. Universal suffrage was just a form; the multiparty system turned into partisanism and nepotism; the parliamentary house became a brawling room for a few politicians ... Instead of solving China's problems, imitative Western-style democracy had more fragmented China's political ecology and ended in failure.

The Russian Revolution erupting in 1917 showed the Chinese a new choice of a development road and brought the Communist Party of China into being. Instead of abandoning "Mr. De", the nascent party bestowed new content upon it — a democracy not only for a minority or for personal liberation, but also for the vast majority of the people and the liberation of the nation. The Chinese

Communists, represented by Mao Zedong, further transformed the Western concept of democracy into a catchy Chinese-style expression, that is, "People are the masters of the country."

The CPC recognizes the value of democracy and considers "democracy to be a good thing,"[2] but like many modern Western thinkers, the CPC believes that democracy is only a relatively reasonable institutional arrangement to achieve the country's long-term political goals, the realization of which can be diverse and must be based on its specific national conditions. History and reality have repeatedly proved that China cannot simply copy Western democracy, let alone promote Western democracy by "cutting the feet to fit the shoes". China's democracy should be based on its own historical and cultural traditions, and basic national conditions, which means to take the road of Chinese-style democracy, that is, the "Chinese Democratic Road".[3]

Deng Xiaoping put forward in the 1980s that it was crucial to evaluate a country's political system, structure and policies by assessing three facets: first, whether the political situation of the country is stable; second, whether the people's unity and livelihood are improved; and third, whether the productivity can be sustained.[4]

Based on the national conditions, contemporary China has formed a democratic political system characterized by the Communist Party's leadership, the people mastering the country and ruling the country by law. China's political elites believe that blindly imitating democracy would not help in achieving real democracy or developing the economy, but could only throw a state into chaos. Instead of democratizing the country for the sake of democracy, China aims to achieve good governance through democracy and take a development path suiting China's national conditions and prioritizing the interests of the people.

The advantages and disadvantages of a political system are often reflected in the actual effect of national governance. Since China onset the process of reform and opening-up in 1978, the country's GDP has grown 9.5 percent yearly on average, becoming the second largest economy in the world; Chinese people's livelihood has improved dramatically, with more than 700 million people being lifted out of poverty … Facing the great achievement made by China, the Western countries have to admit that China's political system owns huge advantages in national governance, economic development, livelihood improvement and talents election.

In 2008, when China hosted the Olympic Games, then-Chinese ambassador to the United Kingdom Fu Ying told British reporters that one of China's greatest achievements was that the country had solved the problem of feeding 1.3 billion people. For such a populous country like China, eating has always been a focus of political topics. In its long history, around the ability to solve the problem of eating, different dynasties rose and fell in succession. Now China has achieved food self-sufficiency within one generation, which is a remarkable achievement.[5]

According to an article titled "What's Gone Wrong with Democracy" published by *The Economist* in March 2014, China has been doubling living standards roughly every decade for the past 30 years. The Chinese leadership can effectively solve important issues concerning the country's construction in a few years, while other countries may spend decades to solve the same issues. For example, China spent only two years to make its pension system cover 240 million villagers, a number that is much bigger than the total population covered by the U.S. pension system.

To turn a good political system into good national governance, it needs an effective executive body, which in China is represented by the strong and revolutionary ruling party. British scholar Martin Jacques wrote in his book, *When China Rules the World*, that Chinese government is quite qualified, as it has proved its extraordinary succession and is able to conduct self-reform in an admirable way. Since the establishment of the People's Republic of China, such kind of reformation had occurred twice: during the time of Mao Zedong when the CPC set up a new government and united China; and during the time of reform and opening-up when the party renewed itself and regained vigor in leading the country's economic transformation. [6]

The CPC's mechanism to select talents is appreciated as the most effective human resource management system, the aim of which is to choose the most excellent leadership to steer national development. In October 2013, before the Third Plenary Session of the Eighteenth CPC Central Committee, the video *How Leaders are Made* went viral on the Internet. According to the video, Chinese officials need to go through long-term training before becoming leaders of China, like the process of training a *kungfu* master. In China, cadres are graded and have to work generally from the bottom before getting promoted at different administrative levels including town, county, province, etc. For each of the more than 7 million cadres, the odds of getting promoted to a ministerial-level cadre are only one out of 14,000, and the average time required is at least 23 years. The video also mentioned that the current Chinese leader Xi had worked from China's lowest administrative level equivalent to the European and American community level to the level of county and city. He was then gradually promoted to be provincial leader of Fujian, Zhejiang and Shanghai among others, to vice president of the state, later to the party's general secretary, and finally to president of the country. During his over 40 years' experience of at least 16 times of important work adjustments, Xi has managed areas with an accumulated population of more than 150 million people.

As is pointed out by some western media, Canadian Sinologist Daniel A. Bell said that China's political meritocracy can select leaders not only with extraordinary capability but also with long-term vision and overall consciousness, which enable them to make persuasive political judgment. Political meritocracy better suits big countries like China as it can effectively "remedy the key flaws of electoral democracy."

There is a Chinese proverb "You only know if the shoes fit by wearing them yourself." Whether China's political system works, the Chinese themselves are the most qualified to make the judgment. More than 80 percent of Chinese were satisfied with their country's development direction, according to an annual survey published by the Pew Research Center in 2017. As China's economical and political status has risen internationally, the national pride of young people aged above 20 and 30 has grown gradually.

The *Wall Street Journal* commented that Chinese young people no longer worship everything foreign and the Chinese feel they are moving on the right track. According to a report released by the Economist Intelligence Unit on November 12, 2018, China is the most optimistic country in the world, with 91.4 percent of its citizens believing their country will become a better place in the next decade.

Regarding the road and mode of national development, Chinese leaders have always advocated that no country should set its own development path as the authorized one, let alone impose its own development path on others, just as an old saying goes: "All roads lead to Rome." But for some Westerners, evaluating the pros and cons of a country's political system and level of governance depends only on whether the country has implemented Western democracy, and the so-called criterion for democracy is only to see whether the population has universal suffrage or whether there is a multiparty system in the country. Based on this simplistic and dogmatic understanding of democracy, some in the West have arbitrarily and wrongly put a "non-democratic" hat on China, claiming that China is on the path of "authoritarianism."

In the view of Martin Jacques, it is definitely wrong for the West to evaluate China mainly, sometimes even only, based on Western criteria, which would easily become excuses for refusing to understand and respect the wisdom and specialty contained in other countries' culture, history and tradition. In fact, when the West judges China with its own "democratic criteria," it implies the stereotype that the Western democratic system is the best and other countries can realize political modernization only by learning from the West. The "Western-centered theory" totally ignores the restlessness and chaos in countries which were thrown into turmoil after adopting Western democracy.

Some Latin American countries have long been troubled by issues of fragile political parties, a flawed electoral system and military interference in politics since they imported Western democracy in the 1970s. Similar circumstances have also occurred in some African countries, which saw terrible conflicts, wars and economic depression rather than economic prosperity, political stability and realization of people's rights after they accepted Western democracy and started the multiparty ruling system in the 1980s. In the 21st century, countries such as Afghanistan and Iraq, where Western countries exported democracy by force, failed to achieve stable social development with Western-style elections. They instead suffered from exacerbated confrontations and conflicts between different religious and ethnic groups, plunging into turmoil and leading to the rise of the extremist group Islamic State.

Statistics showed that nearly 100 countries transformed from "Authoritarian Regime" to "Democratic Regime" in the 1990s. However, only fewer than 20 countries have successfully achieved "democratic transformation"[7] till now. Some are actually in a state of anarchy. The failure of Western democracy in many developing countries started to make Western scholars recognize that the path to democracy should be taken step by step, and people's political right should be realized and developed gradually. Even in the United States, the so-called exemplar of democracy, electoral rights to African-Americans and other ethnic minorities hadn't been granted until the Voting Rights Act of 1965 outlawed literacy tests before voting. That process took 350 years, before which, in the early colonial times, only white adults who had lands could vote.

Reviewing modern Western society, people can see that democracy featuring general election is facing unprecedented crises. Shortly after the end of the Cold War in 1992, American political scientist Yoshihiro Francis Fukuyama threw out the conclusion of so-called "the end of history", believing that liberal democracies may signal the end point of humanity's sociocultural evolution, while the bourgeois under liberal democracy could be the "Last Man". But more than 20 years have passed, and the conclusion of "the end of history" has proved its own incorrectness. In his paper published in 2014, Fukuyama pointed out that the U.S. democratic system has come to a deadlock because of interest groups' control over the decision-making process and the two parties' abuse of their veto power.[8] In 2016, Donald Trump was elected as the U.S. president, aggravating the polarization of the country's politics, which gave Chinese scholar Wang Jisi a "strong sense of disillusionment" with the United States. "When I first went to the United States in 1984, the American political struggle was relatively rational and civilized. Now as the liberals' accusations against Trump often turn into personal attacks describing him as a worthless person, and so does he scold the opposition, the society begins to show antagonism, disgust and hatred," he told Chinese media.[9]

II. The Complex Myth to Change China

Some Western politicians have always held the illusion that China will eventually move toward Western-style multiparty parliamentary politics in the process of reform and opening-up. In recent years, especially since the 18th National Congress of the CPC in 2012, this illusion has gradually been shattered during the process of China's successful practice of its own road. At the same time, the United States has been increasingly worried that China's political system and development path will challenge American-style democracy and the market economy model it boasts, thus impacting the post-Cold War political and economic order that the United States is trying to dominate. Henry Kissinger, revealed that for neoconservatives and other radicals, "getting along with China is no longer a strategic issue, but an issue of how to change the way China governs itself."

The history of Sino-U.S. relations in the past century shows that a kind of missionary emotion has always influenced the American political elites on the country's policy tendency towards China. The United States believes itself to be a unique country, like a city on a hill overlooking the other ones; it has the right and responsibility to rule the world, and it has the obligation to "teach" China to abide by basic "moral principles." In fact, religious zeal and economic interests have jointly promoted the establishment and development of early Sino-U.S. relations since the American merchant ship, The Empress of China, arrived at Guangzhou in 1784 and opened the history of modern Sino-U.S. exchanges.[10] Today, the era of missionaries has long ended, but the complex myth of changing China continues.

In 1978, China began the process of reform and opening-up. The United States made a self-evident assumption that the opening up of the economy would become the forerunner for Western-style democracy to enter China, and then "a democratic China just like what the United States assumes" would come into shape. In the spring of 2000, U.S. Congress debated and voted on the bill of China's entering the World Trade Organization (WTO). In order to convince Congress, then-President Bill Clinton made a careful preparation for his speech. He said that through entrance to the WTO, China would not only agree to import more products, but also agree to import one of the most cherished values of democracy — economic freedom.[11] In Clinton's imagination, after China's accession to the WTO, President Woodrow Wilson's "Democracy Vision" could be achieved in the country.

President Clinton's self-confidence came from his observation of the international environment. Victory in the Cold War has cheered the American politicians, and the "end of socialism history" has become the universal conclusion of Western society. After the disintegration of the Soviet Union and the drastic changes in Eastern Europe, some strategists in the United States believed that China was on the verge of territorial secession, political collapse or democratic revolution, and it was China's turn to fall. Zbigniew Brzezinski asserted in his book *The Grand Failure* that socialism would be a complete failure by the end of the 20th century. However, today's people have seen that China has not become "the second Soviet Union"; on the contrary, in fewer than 40 years it has grown into the world's second largest economy. China has developed faster than what Western people expected, and its modernization road has its own characteristics, which is different from the former Soviet Union system. What is more, it is also distinguished from Western ideas. While the hawks in America are feeling disillusioned, they believe the reason why the United States has established diplomatic relations with China and allowed China to develop without limitation is that the United States has been "deceived" and "misled" by China.

What caused the failure of Westernizing China? Is it because of China's "intentional misleading" or the United States' own "strategic misjudgment"? Perhaps history can provide a just answer. During the War of Liberation of China, a U.S. observer mission submitted a large number of objective military and political reports to their government[12]. They believed that the CPC was becoming stronger and stronger, and opposed the U.S. government's one-sided support for the Kuomintang, because the United States couldn't provide indefinite support to a regime that has bankrupted in politics. They even prophesied that no matter how many supplies they provided to the Kuomintang government, the people who called themselves communists would one day take over the country. At that time, U.S. representative Joseph Stilwell also wrote in his diary that he made the judgment about the Kuomintang and the Communist Party based on everything he had seen: Kuomintang has become corrupted, neglected its duty and chaos; economic embarrassment, rigorous taxation, empty talk, taking no action, hoarding black market and opening commerce with the enemy are all done by Kuomintang. The Communist Party's guiding principles — which were reducing taxes, reducing rents, cutting interest rates, and raising production levels and living standards — have been practiced. However, these sensible conclusions and propositions failed to fundamentally influence and change the U.S. policy toward China. Under the guidance of overconfidence gained since World War II and the thinking of the Cold War toward the Soviet Union, the U.S. government had determined to help the Chiang Kai-shek regime fight against the CPC, and finally both the United States' policy toward China and the Chiang regime failed together. As a result, the United States has also set off a discussion on the topic of who was to blame for the United States losing China. The China experts in the U.S. State Department also became scapegoats for explaining why the United States lost China, and victims of McCarthyism[13], simply because they had positively evaluated the CPC or predicted the failure of the Kuomintang.

Pride and prejudice have replaced reason and foresight, which has repeatedly caused the United States to make strategic misjudgments about China. Statistics show that as many as six major strategic misjudgments about China have been made by the U.S. government over the past 70 years since the end of World War II, including which of the two parties, the Kuomintang and the CPC, could win the leadership, whether China would send troops to the Korean War, and whether China would become the "second Soviet Union." American political scientist Hans J. Morgenthau (1904-1980) pointed out that the miscalculation and wrong decision of the United States on China policy were rooted in two types of "political patients" in the U.S. leadership. In the preface of the book *America's Failure in China, 1941-50*, he said neurotic patients believe that two plus two equals five, while psychos know that two plus two equals four, but they are unhappy about the result. When it comes to China, the Americans fall into two categories, one with neuropathy and the other with psycho illness. Only a handful of people whose voices are almost inaudible dare to face history with a calm and objective attitude. By doing so, the Americans need to face up to themselves, reveal their own misjudgments and wrong actions, and thus discover that the real reason for "losing China" is neither negligence nor treasonous behavior of a group of scapegoats that can be identified, but the Americans themselves.

American scholars Kurt M. Campbell and Ely Ratner wrote in their co-authored article "The China Reckoning" (published in *Foreign Affairs* magazine, March-April, 2018) that the United States always overestimates its ability in determining China's development path. They wrote that, after the victory of World War II, the pride of the Americans being almighty made them neglect that what they were facing is a civilization-state that experienced rise and fall and foreign invasions but still lasted for nearly 5,000 years without interruption. Why does the United States repeatedly fail to understand China, cannot see China clearly or make right judgments about China? In British scholar Martin Jacques' view, the key is that the Western countries ignore the integrity and continuity of Chinese history and culture. He published an article in the Los Angeles Times entitled "Understanding China — the West has gotten it wrong on China for decades", in which he wrote: "even as it (China) embraces a market economy, it has shunned Western-style freedoms; there has been an underlying assumption that the process of modernization would inevitably lead to Westernization, yet modernization is not just shaped by markets, competition and technology but by history and culture, and Chinese history and culture are very different from that of any Western nation-state; if we are to understand China, we must move beyond the compass of Western reality and experience and the body of concepts that has grown up to explain that history."[14]

The Western-centered theory makes it difficult for the United States to judge China's future direction based on China's political and cultural tradition and the historical reality that China is facing. As a result, it underestimates or even ignores the Chinese people's national self-esteem and subject consciousness of transforming their own destiny in seeking freedom and liberation, thus the West fall into the myth of changing China. On July 25, 2018, Chinese Ambassador to the United States Cui Tiankai was invited to attend the activities of the Carnegie Endowment for International Peace, where he said: "It is an illusion to change China. I don't think China and the United States can really change each other like what some people advocate. China has its own history, culture, politics and economic system. No matter what happens to China, it is determined by China's long history. No country can truly change China. Changing China should not be the goal of any country's policy towards China, including the U.S. government. I believe that this is not the policy goal of successive U.S. presidents towards China. I once talked to Dr. (Henry) Kissinger about this issue and he told me that changing China was never the original intention of him and President Nixon to open the door to Sino-U.S. relations."[15]

The famous American Chinese historian Jonathan D. Spence's view in his book, to *Change China*, is quite intriguing: Westerners came to China with an attitude of supremacy, and they think that their goals are lofty and their suggestions are urgently needed by China, believing that they are the ones superior to the Chinese. If China questioned the objectives set by them and did not accept their suggestions, they would be perplexed or shamed into anger. They did not realize that the Chinese viewed the bilateral relationship from a contractual point of view and retained the right to terminate the agreement as an employer. This misunderstanding could lead to serious consequences. Taking the United States as an example, it played an active role as advisors during the late Qing Dynasty and the Republic of China, but it also had the argument of being betrayed by China and losing China. Actually, the United States has not been betrayed. It only repeated the mistakes of the past. The United States should not regard China as its dependency, in the same way as Roman Catholicism treats Europe, Britain treats its colonies and the Soviet Union treats its allies.[16]

It is said that the West's predictions and judgments about China may have succeeded only twice. The first time was Napoleon's impression of China. He compared China to a sleeping lion, which once awake would shock the world. It seems that this prediction is correct. China, the sleeping lion, has really woken up and amazed the world, but it is a peaceful, amiable and civilized lion. The second was from Nixon. He believed that the modern world could not isolate the red China and personally embarked on an ice-breaking journey to open Sino-U.S. relations, becoming a person who created history. Today's U.S. politicians are still enjoying the strategic dividend of this ice-breaking trip.

At present, Sino-U.S. relations are heading into a new historical crossroad. The Sino-U.S. trade war is triggering the world's worries about another Cold War. It is concerning world peace and prosperity for China and the United States to make a rational and responsible prejudgment of each other's strategic direction. Analysts said that it is very likely to become a major strategic misjudgment for the United States in the 21st century to regard China as a new Cold War opponent.

III. Misconception on Nationalism

There are no lack of melodramas as human civilization unfolds a process of collision, communication and integration. For a country as huge as China, its rising process, like the mountain-making movement, is certain to bring profound changes to the landscape of the world's civilization. As a result, the Western world, which has dominated the course of human history over the recent 500-plus years, will inevitably undergo an adaptation process, at the early stages of which prejudices, misunderstandings, conflicts, fears and precautions are unavoidable concomitants.

In 2017, *War Wolf II*, a Chinese military action movie, topped the box office of the Chinese film market, sparking worldwide attention. The phenomenal movie told the story of a former Chinese soldier who couldn't forget duty when he was not in the service, and returned to the battlefield in an African country to rescue Chinese nationals while he could have safely evacuated at first during a rebellion. At the end of the film, the camera slowly zoomed in on a Chinese passport, on which several lines of Chinese characters were typed: "Citizens of the People's Republic of China: When you are in danger overseas, don't give up! Remember, behind you, there is a strong motherland." This scene ignited a strong sense of national honor and pride among the Chinese audience, some of whom even spontaneously rose and started singing the Chinese national anthem in the theater.

However, from such a movie, British media did not see patriotism of the Chinese people, but rather, they believed that the whole film is full of nationalist sentiments, which met the rising tide of nationalism in China and thus made the film such a hit. This kind of comment may not be regarded as a problem for Chinese people, because they see no difference between patriotism and nationalism and believe it is natural for a nation to be proud of its present development achievements after decades of oppression by other powers. However, nationalism is often regarded by the West as a noxious ideology, and the vicious development of nationalism has become the main trigger of many wars ravaging modern Europe. Therefore, when a Chinese film is labeled as nationalism, it is easy to guess what kind of associations the film will arouse among the Western audience.

The rise of a "non-Western" power could understandably incur complex mentality of the Western countries. This kind of mentality partly comes from the unknown; the rapid rise of China leaves the Western countries little time to collect enough information to predict China's future direction. It partly comes from fear; based on their own history of conducting colonial expansion with violence, the Western powers tend to believe that the enhancement of China's national strength is bound to draw forth its ambition of expansion. Reviewing the past is the best way to predict the future. It is widely acknowledged that the peaceful attributes of the Chinese people derived from the farming civilization, and the logic that a rising power is bound to seek hegemony has never been applicable to China. The so-called growing nationalism of China in the Western context is actually the national dignity and patriotism of the Chinese people after the country washes away more than 100 years of humiliation, which differs from mentalities of revenge, exclusion or even hegemony.

From 1405 to 1433 in China's Ming Dynasty, under orders from the emperor, famous Chinese navigator Zheng sailed his fleets to the Western Ocean seven times. Before Zheng's departure, the emperor ordered that the fleets must not bully the small or the weak, and share the blessings of peace with others. As a pioneer during the Age of Discovery, wherever Zheng's fleet went, "there is no military aggression, no oppression of people; the civilization of rites and music was performed and publicized among foreign countries;"[17] they read the imperial edicts to other peoples, and offered seals and silk ribbons, crowns, and other gifts to the monarchs of different countries, expressing good wishes to "share the blessings of peace" with all countries; they gave the Chinese almanac to the tributary countries to spread the knowledge of seasons and climate, and share civilized norms including the ethics, etiquette and customs of the Chinese people with countries they visited. Compared with European navigators who aimed to develop trade routes and find new continents or gold, the purpose of Zheng's voyages was to appease other countries, promote peaceful diplomacy, and spread the seeds of ritual and musical civilization. Professor Joseph Needham of the University of Cambridge said the Eastern navigators from China are calm and gentle; they forgive and forget their former enmities, and never pose threats against others, generous and hospitable; they are fully armed, but never conquer the aliens, nor build a stronghold.[18]

In history, China has been upholding principles of "earning the world's admiration with morality," "treating countries afar with kindness" and "offering more while asking for less" in diplomatic activities. Even in Sunzi's Art of War, some military strategies have also embodied the philosophy of peace and harmony, such as the strategy of "those who subdue the enemy without fighting are the best of all." The thinking of "governing the country with no violence" has been deeply embedded in the Chinese people. Regarding the peaceful nature of the Chinese civilization, a famous Japanese scholar Daisaku Ikeda once pointed out that the Chinese are not the people who have ambitions of conquering others, but rather the conservatives who just want peace and prosperity for their country. In fact, China will never beat others to the draw if it is not infringed on at first. In modern times, all the wars related to China so far, including the Opium War, the Sino-Japanese War and the Korean War, can be regarded as self-defense.[19]

Building colonies, battling to expand sphere of influence and waging wars of aggression had been the rising paths of some great powers in modern history. Especially in the 20th century, the pursuit of hegemony and military confrontation has dragged humanity into the catastrophe of the two World Wars. China was also one of the victims. With the lessons of history and the tradition of Chinese civilization, China is determined to take a development path which is different from the Western ones. In 2011, the Chinese government released the White Paper on China's Peaceful Development to the world, indicating that based on its thousands of years of historical and cultural traditions, its understanding of economic globalization, international relations and changes in the international security landscape in the 21st century, as well as its recognition of the common interests and values of mankind, China is committed to breaking the traditional rising model of the Western powers and choosing peaceful development and win-win cooperation as its basic approaches to achieving national modernization, participating in international affairs and handling international relations. The Communist Party of China (CPC) has always made it its mission to make new and greater contributions to mankind. During the 19th CPC National Congress in 2017, Chinese President Xi Jinping once again announced that China will adhere to the path of peaceful development and promote the building of a community with a shared future for mankind.

However, even historical traditions and policy announcements don't appear to be convincing enough to free the Western conservative forces from strategic bias against China. Some hawkish officials in the United States claim that they do not believe in the strategic guarantees made by the Chinese white paper, and even worry that China's thinking of keeping low-key development is just a temporary trick against the backdrop that China is still far behind the United States, rather than a long-term strategic plan. Treating China as not a member of the same clan, Western countries like the United States are either making a profit off China, or blocking its development with sanctions, or slandering and demonizing it, and even concocting various distorted arguments to confuse the public. For example, they will pleasantly predict the "Collapse of China"once the Chinese economy encounters twists and turns, hoping to see China following the footsteps of the former Soviet Union; and if China's economy is showing an upward trend, those countries will conjure up the "Threat of China" so as to build a united front to contain China. In short, they cannot just peacefully sit by and watch China's development without worrying about gains and losses. As a result, the long-standing patriotism of the Chinese people is often misinterpreted intentionally or not by the West as "extreme nationalism" deliberately incited by the government "in order to strengthen the centralized rule."

In the late 1980s and early 1990s, the Western group headed by the United States still imposed severe economic sanctions against China in an attempt to intensify China's domestic contradictions and strike a final blow to this major socialist country. Former Chinese foreign minister Qian Qichen said in his memoir *Ten Episodes in China's Diplomacy* that during his 10 years as foreign minister, the most difficult time of Chinese diplomacy he ever experienced was the period from the late 1980s to the early 1990s. At that time, the international situation facing China underwent a sudden change, Western governments announced a series of sanctions against China, and various political forces set off anti-China waves in the world for different purposes.[20]

External containment evokes the nation's historical memory of being oppressed and greatly stimulates the patriotism of the Chinese people, which, paradoxically, in the view of former U.S. CIA official Michael Pillsbury, is also a conspiracy of the Chinese "hawks". The government starts to weaken the ideology of communism and turn to extreme nationalism to ensure the continuation of the regime, he believed. In Western context, extreme nationalism often leads to negative associations due to its close connection with Nazi Germany in World War II. Mistaking Chinese patriotism stirred up by sanctions of Western countries for "extreme nationalism" is due to either political motives to incite Western countries' hostility towards China, or "selective loss of memory" about China's modern history.

The Chinese nation created splendid civilizations in ancient times, but it fell far behind in modern times. In 1840, when the Opium War broke out, China began to lose its full sovereignty and dignity as an independent country, and embarked on a semi-colonial road subject to bullying and manipulation of foreign colonists. In 1900, the Eight-Power alliance invaded China, making it the first time in human history that all the imperialist countries in the world united to jointly wage a war against another country. Since then, the Eight-Power alliance occupied China's capital Beijing for a year and implemented zoning regulation, commanding residents to hang the national flag of the invaders. This humiliation deeply hurt the Chinese.

Regarding the joint sanctions imposed by Western powers, Deng Xiaoping, the chief architect of China's reform and opening-up, had a meaningful word. "I am a Chinese and I know the history of foreign aggression against China. When I heard that the Western Seven-Power Summit decided to sanction China, the history of the Eight-Power aggression against China in 1900 immediately came into my mind. Except Canada, the other six countries of the summit, together with Russia and Austria, were the eight countries that organized the invading troops that year. We must gain some knowledge of the Chinese history, which is a spiritual impetus for China's development," Deng said on April 7, 1990, when he met with entrepreneurs from Thailand.[21]

China has never been an aggressive country posing threats to other nations; rather, passively responding to external aggression and oppression is an iconic way of the Chinese nation to express its national consciousness. In the 1980s, the ideological movement brought by the reform and opening-up enabled the Chinese to see a bigger world and left most Chinese people with a good impression of the Western countries. Learning from the West has become the voice of the entire Chinese society. However, since the early 1990s, due to the joint suppression and containment of the Western group against China, the people's illusion with the West was shattered. Many scholars at that time began to reflect on Western civilization and Sino-Western relations, publishing a series of books with the theme of saying "no" to the United States. Such a shift in attitude toward the West stems from the passively responsive nature of the Chinese national consciousness. Japanese philosopher Daisaku Ikeda once said that Chinese nationalism occurred as an unavoidable response to the aggression of foreign powers, including Japan, since the Opium War. It's a better explanation and I think that nationalism is just an aspect of China's response, Ikeda said, adding that, overally speaking, China is a vigorous promoter of cosmopolitanism and Chineseism. [22]

Since ancient times, "living side by side with other nations in perfect harmony" and "treating the whole world as one community" have always been the ultimate moral pursuit of Chinese Confucianists. Until modern times, when the whole nation had been put into peril since the closed door of ancient China was crushed by Westerners during the Opium War, the Chinese began to think about the historical proposition of building a modern nation-state. From the collapse of the Qing Dynasty to the building of the Republic, from the May Fourth Movement to the fighting of warlords, from the Northern Expedition to the War of Resistance against Japanese Aggression, with efforts of generations, the Chinese people have finally established the New China at the cost of tens of millions of people's lives. Later, it experienced many twists and turns, and finally, 40 years after the reform and opening-up, it has established its status as a true world power and is restoring its deserved status in the history of human civilization. Nowadays, the "backward theory" about China, concluded from the perspective of Western modernization, has gradually become marginalized in the country, and the growing national strength and prosperous social outlook have made the Chinese more confident. Their recognition of the nation and the country has never been as strong as it is today. For Western countries, such kind of national pride, which could be continuously enhanced with the improvement of national strength, is called patriotism; however, when it comes to China, it is misunderstood as "nationalism that may be out of control."

Under the CPC leadership, the ancient and unique civilization has been revived in fewer than 70 years, earning appreciation from all around the world. The new path of modernization for late-developing countries that China opened up based on its history and national conditions has not only created a miracle of its own, but also produced a huge positive spillover effect on world development. Against such a backdrop, various slanders against China have emerged. The Belt and Road Initiative that China proposed for the building of a new platform of global development has been accused of becoming a new tool for China to pursue geographical expansion; cooperation between China and Africa has also been vilified for enveloping; the development financing for infrastructure construction is described as a "debt trap," etc. In short, the West's fear of China may come from its vigilance about China's strong national strength on the one hand, while on the other, there is another possible cause for its deeper anxiety, which is that the new development path and cultural value that China is showing the world may rock the dominant Western civilization.

"Sharp Power", another concept made up by the West in the framework of the China Threat Theory, has recently been used to describe the growing international influence and appeal of China.[23] Pan Wei, a Chinese scholar, believes that China's success makes the world re-examine the prevailing knowledge about human progress, and poses challenges to the two-dimensional division of "state and society" in Western sociology, "democracy and autocracy" in political science, and "planned economy and market economy." The Chinese school is taking shape. Zhu Yunhan, another Chinese scholar, believes that China's success heralds a reversal of historical trends, creating a larger thinking space for non-Western societies to make a choice about their own social and value system. Therefore, "making progress" does not necessarily mean learning from the West, and resuming one's own cultural traditions does not necessarily mean "outdated." The external constraints imposed by the Western world on the non-Western countries are getting less and less.[24]

Undoubtedly, under the background of major changes in the balance of world power and the rise of developing countries and emerging market countries, the rejuvenation of Chinese civilization will bring profound and fundamental changes to the world in many fields including economy, politics, culture, science and technology, which, in essence, represents the progress of human civilization. China also has a clear sense of self-consciousness about its historical role. Therefore, it pays great attention to monitoring the interaction process with the world, making timely and clear policy statements, providing sufficient information for eliminating strategic misjudgments, and allowing the world to get a better understanding of China. In fact, from countless official reports and white papers, it is not difficult to see China's policy structure and development direction, and make correct strategic judgments. For example, China has repeatedly stressed that the goal of "achieving the great rejuvenation of the Chinese nation" does not mean to engage in narrow and exclusive nationalism, or to assume hegemony, but to inspire the Chinese nation to be confident, independent and self-reliant, accelerate its own development process and strive to make a greater contribution to human development. However, before crossing the "prejudice curtain" of the West and getting correctly interpreted, these positive signals have many challenges to address.

[1] Xi Jinping: *The Governance of China* (Volume 2), Foreign Language Press, Dec. 2017, 1st edition, p.29.

[2] Keping, Y., "Democracy is A Good Thing", *Journal of Theoretical Reference*, 2007,(9), p.30.

[3] Ning, F., *China's Democracy Path*, China Social Sciences Press, 2018, p.1.

[4] *Selected Works of Deng Xiaoping*, 1993, p.213.

[5] Ying, F., *See the World*, CITIC Press, 2018, p.293.

[6] Jacques, M., *When China Rules the World*, 2016, p.423.

[7] Carothers, T., "The End of the Transition Paradigm." *Journal of Democracy*, 2002, 13(1), pp. 5-21.

[8] Fukuyama, F., America in Decay The Sources of Political Dysfunction, https://www.foreignaffairs.com/articles/united-states/2014-08-18/america-decay.

[9] *Fang Wang Jisi: Meiguo fadong maoyizhan bu shi wei le likai zhongguo [Leaving China is not the reason why the United States launches Trade War], FT(Chinese)* https://www.ftchinese.com/story/001079777?full=y&archive.

[10] Xiaodong, X., Beginning of Sino-U.S. Trade — the Whole Process of "Empress of China" Coming to China. The World and Chongqing, 2014, (10) , pp.15-19.

[11] Clinton, B., "By joining the W.T.O., China is not simply agreeing to import more of our products; it is agreeing to import one of democracy's most cherished values: economic freedom," 2000.

[12] In the second half of 1944, a total of 18 U.S. military observation teams arrived in Yan'an in two batches. With the official name "The U.S. Army's China-Burma-India Theater in Yan'an Observation Group," it consisted of US military officers, diplomats, doctors and professional technicians, and was regarded as "the beginning of formal contact between the U.S. and the CPC leaders".

[13] Three months after the founding of new China, senator McCarthy, an "anti-communist fighter," made a speech accusing that the state department harbored more than 200 communists. The danger that the United States is going to face is not the possibility of foreign aggression, but the betrayal of certain people who are favored by the state. He accused that the entire State Department was riddled with the Communist Party. From 1950 to 1954, he maliciously and arbitrarily

persecuted suspected Communists, democratic progressives and even people with different opinions, causing a large number of defamation cases, which was known as McCarthyism.

[14] Jacques, M., "Understanding China: the West has gotten it wrong on China for decades", *Los Angeles Times*, 2009.

[15] http://world.people.com.cn/n1/2018/0727/c1002-30174854.html

[16] Spence, J., *To Change China: Western Advisers in China,* p. 292.

[17] *Family Information about Zheng He*, Shanghai Jiao Tong University Press, 1985, p.2.

[18] *Family Information about Zheng He,* Shanghai Jiao Tong University Press, 1985, p.2.

[19] Ikeda, D.& Toynbee, A., Forecast the 21st Century:A Dialogue Between Daisaku Ikeda and Arnold J.Toynbee.

[20] Qichen, Q., *Ten Episodes in China's Diplomacy*, World Affairs Press.

[21] The Chronicle of the Communist Party of China (1990), retrieved from http://www.gov.cn/test/2007-09/05/content_737583.htm

[22] *Family Information about Zheng He,* Shanghai Jiao Tong University Press, 1985, p.2.

[23] The British *Economist* used an cover article to describe China's "sharp power" in October 2017, claiming China's foreign cultural exchanges are controlled by the government, with the purpose of manipulating the social values and intervening freedom in various cultural fields of Western countries.

[24] Yunhan, Zhu., *The Rise of China and Reorganization of the Global Order,* China Renmin University Press, 2015.

Chapter Five

"Empress of China" and Statue of Liberty

"The Chinese people have always held American entrepreneurship and creativity in high regards."

— Xi Jinping

I. Replicating the "Empress of China"

It has been a dream for Dr. Meng Xingyu, a Boston-based Chinese scholar, to replicate the "Empress of China", the vessel that made the voyage between China and the United States for the first time. Built shortly after America's independence from Britain, the three-masted sailing ship has been obscured by the dust of history, making it difficult to verify its appearance. Dr. Meng often visits the Independence Seaport Museum in Philadelphia for inspiration.

As one of the most authoritative maritime museums in the United States, it contains more details about the Empress of China than any other place. Here, the first letter between the two countries carried by the Empress of China as well as a Chinese painted fan with the only known portrayal of the vessel are on display. The fan depicts the Empress of China anchoring at the ancient harbor of Whampoa in Canton with a technique used in Chinese paintings, and shows the first impression that the United States has made on China.

According to *The Empress of China* published by Independence Seaport Museum in 1984, the vessel was initially built for the U.S. Navy, and renamed after being refitted for commercial purposes. The name "Empress of China" probably came from the reverence towards queens in Anglo-Saxon culture, and reflected Americans' fantasy of the faraway oriental giant. It should be noted that due to a lack of knowledge of China, the letter brought by Captain John Green was not assigned to be submitted to a certain Chinese official. Instead, the letter started with "Most Serene, Serene, most puissant, puissant, high, illustrious, noble, honorable, venerable, wise and prudent Emperors, Kings, Republicks, Princes, Dukes, Earls, Barons, Lords, Burgomasters, Councillors, as also Judges, Officers, Justiciaries & Regents of all the good Cities and places whether ecclesiastical or secular who shall see these patents or hear them read[2]."

After a six-month-long voyage, the Empress of China arrived in Canton, one of the starting points of the maritime silk road, in late August 1784, when the Whampoa harbor was full of commercial vessels from all over the world. In 1757, 27 years before the arrival of the Empress of China, the Qing Dynasty created a policy of single-port trading relations, making Canton the only foreign trade port of the whole empire. During the history of the maritime silk road, Canton has been the only port that has prospered continuously.

According to Dr. Meng, the Empress of China saluted China with 13 guns when she arrived at Whampoa. There were only 13 states in America at that time while China only allowed 13 factories to deal with foreign trade. 13 factories and 13 guns, what a coincidence!

When the American vessel sailed from New York to China in 1784, the

Chinese Emperor Qianlong was busy inspecting his unprecedented prosperous empire. On the other side of the Earth, the American Revolutionary War came to an end on Jan. 14 of that year, and the former colony declared its independence from Britain as the United States of America. Economic woes troubled the newborn country; American foreign trade was blocked by Britain, the maritime superpower. To obtain economic independence, the United States had to explore a new trade system while China, an empire with great productivity and consumption potential, became a natural trade partner.

European countries dared not to approach the United States under great pressure from Britain. In order to solve this difficulty, U.S. Superintendent of Finance Robert Morris wrote a letter to Secretary of Foreign Affairs John Jay in November 1783, proposing to send a vessel to China to seek trade opportunities. On Feb. 22, 1784, George Washington's birthday, the Empress of China departed from New York amid cheers and expectations.

Upon its arrival in Canton, the vessel was warmly welcomed by the Chinese people. "Our being the first American ship that had ever visited China, it was some time before the Chinese could fully comprehend the distinction between us and Englishmen. They styled us the New People; and when, by the map we conveyed to them an idea of the extent of our country, with its present and increasing population, they were not highly pleased at the prospect of so considerable a market for the productions of their own empire," the ship's all-important supercargo Samuel Shaw wrote in his journal, which was given as a present to Guangzhou years later.

Breaking through the economic blockade imposed by Britain, the Empress of China started a new period of foreign trade and provided timely help to the newborn country. The U.S. Congress praised the voyage publicly to promote trade with China while newspapers covered it extensively, praising it as a "foresighted and fruitful" trip. Promoted by the government and promising lucrative profits, trade with China developed rapidly. China became the second-largest trade partner of the United States in the 1790s, only behind Britain. Thanks to the capital earned through trade with China, the United States accumulated a great amount of wealth and broke through the blockades imposed by European countries. Before her second voyage to China, the vessel's crew received a letter from President George Washington, who ordered porcelain and nankeen fabric for his wife. The order demonstrated the first couple's affection for Chinese products and of course promoted bilateral trade.

The Empress of China returned to New York on May 15, 1785 with Chinese cargoes. In front of an excited crowd in Manhattan, Captain Green finished the 15-month-long voyage with a 13-gun salute. Shaw's journal became a hit through the country once it was published in Boston. Media called the voyage "a milestone in American commercial history." Cargoes onboard were soon sold out, including a teapot painted with Chinese flying dragons which was said to have been acquired by President Washington for his collection.

Dr. Meng's idea of replicating the Empress of China came from her visit to the replica of the Mayflower. On Sept. 6, 1620, the ship carried 102 Puritans from Plymouth, England to America, where they established the first colony. It became a cultural icon after the independence of the United States and was replicated by the city of Plymouth in the United States in 1975 as part of an exhibition. Dr. Meng understands that due to a lack of money, manpower and technology, replicating the Empress of China is "bound to fail". However, her intention was not just replicating the vessel, but also making people understand the historical background and significance of the Empress of China. "Braveness, fearlessness, communication and cooperation were all good qualities shown by the Chinese and Americans after the Empress of China had reached its destination. The two countries are just like a couple who should review the beginning of their relationship frequently to see how inclusive and supportive they were of each other," Dr. Meng said.

While Dr. Meng had been pursuing her dream of replicating the Empress of China, the Boston-based landscape designer Thomas Paine had been conducting genealogical research to learn more about his family tree.

On Sept. 11, 1809, Paine's great-grandfather John Bryant followed the trail that the Empress of China blazed 25 years ago to visit Whampoa. "I have read Bryant's journal. Its detailed description stunned me," Paine said. Motivated by promoters of the bilateral friendship like Paine, legislators of Massachusetts designated Aug. 28, 2014 as "Guangzhou, Guangdong – Boston, Massachusetts Day" to remember the great achievements their ancestors had made in bilateral trade between the two countries, and to enhance communication with Guangzhou.

II. The Statue of Liberty

There was another symbolic event that took place at New York Harbor exactly a century after the Empress of China had returned to the same site. On June 17, 1885, a French steamer arrived in New York with the disassembled Statue of Liberty, which was warmly welcomed by New Yorkers.

Visitors to the city will never forget the statue standing at New York Harbor. The liberty goddess wears a stola, her head is topped with a crown, and she holds the U.S. Declaration of Independence in her left hand and a torch of liberty in her right. A broken chain lies at her feet as she steps forward. When night falls, the jade green body of the goddess mingles with the orange light of her torch, enhancing the statue's elegance.

The statue was equipped an exterior lighting system in 1916, making it a giant landmark that welcomes visitors and immigrants night and day. She also appears in popular films as the symbol of the United States. She witnessed the moment that Rose returned to her homeland after surviving a shipwreck in the movie *Titanic*. She was the frozen goddess in *The Day After Tomorrow*. She was also the heartbreaking landmark of the new world in *The Legend of 1900*.

Years after the construction of the Statue of Liberty, *The New Colossus*, a sonnet that was written by the poet Emma Lazarus to raise money for the construction, was rediscovered and cast onto the pedestal of the statue. The emotional sonnet with its emphasis on morality and espousing humanitarian values defined the statue as a guide to and provider of freedom, representing hope for the homeless. From the construction of the Statue of Liberty to the end of the 20th century, the number of immigrants that the United States had admitted was over 50 million, which exceeded the populations of most countries in the world. As the most popular destination for immigrants and refugees, the United States gradually developed into the "leader of the Free World" after World War II, and the Statue of Liberty had become an icon of the country.

Franz Kafka had perfectly described the feelings of immigrants when they entered New York Harbor. "A sudden burst of sunshine seemed to illumine the Statue of Liberty, so that he saw it in a new light, although he had sighted it long before. The arm with the sword rose up as if newly stretched aloft, and round the figure blew the free winds of heaven," wrote Kafka in his novel *Amerika*.

The feelings were also shared by some Chinese. "Images of the Statue of Liberty were common in media, and I can imagine her towering figure under the sunshine easily. However, I was still stunned when standing in front of her. How much comfort and inspiration had her welcoming image and darkness-splitting light from her crown brought to those comers!" wrote Zhang Xianzhang early this century.

III. Changing Perceptions

Only a few Chinese have the chance to see the Statue of Liberty and experience the United States. In addition to movies, television plays and news reports, the classroom and textbooks are where most Chinese get their perceptions of the United States. Zhao Mei, an expert on the United States at the Chinese Academy of Social Sciences, analyzed thoughts on teaching the history of foreign countries (including that of the United States), as well as the teaching content and viewpoints of U.S. history in Chinese primary and secondary schools from 1902 to 2003. Her analysis found that since the end of the Qing Dynasty, the evaluation of the United States in the history textbooks of Chinese middle schools has become more rational and objective on the whole, and the understanding of the United States has also been increased.

She found out that from 1902 to the present, China's history textbooks basically showed a positive attitude towards U.S. historical issues before the Civil War, and posited that before the Civil War, the United States was in the stages of developing laissez-faire capitalism. The image of the country during the period was generally positive and progressive. The textbooks' attitude towards U.S. history after the Civil War, however, has changed along with the changes in China's domestic political environment and international status. China's love-hate relationship with the United States is fully demonstrated in the textbook's interpretation of this period in U.S. history: In the late Qing Dynasty, the textbooks considered it as a Western power with both "a Bible and a knife"; during the period of the Republic of China, it was considered a capitalist, imperialistic power; then in the 1950s and 1960s, it was seen as the most dangerous enemy. In the 1970s and 1980s, China regarded it as having the monopoly on capitalism; and in the early 21st century, it was more seen as a developed capitalist country.

Since the end of the Qing Dynasty, the changes of how the United States was perceived and the different interpretations of U.S. history in textbooks have reflected the development of China's American studies in the past 100 years, as well as Chinese people's understanding of the United States. Zhao held the opinion that modern Chinese people's interpretation of the United States was mostly emotional, and cannot be regarded as academic research in a strict sense. George Washington and the American War of Independence led by him became models for the Chinese who were seeking innovation and reforms in China. In 1901, the United States' Declaration of Independence was first translated into Chinese and published in a Chinese newspaper. Washington and Abraham Lincoln were heroes in the eyes of the Chinese. From 1949 to the end of the "Cultural Revolution," most of China's books and reports on the United States exposed and criticized the "sins of U.S. imperialism." In the 1960s, the Chinese media gave some attention to the African-American civil rights movement and considered it part of the world revolution. During this period, the Chinese people's views of the United States were relatively negative. They believed that the United States was a "paper tiger" and "decayed day by day." U.S. President Richard Nixon's visit to China opened the door of China-U.S. relations. The United States no longer appeared only as a wicked power, instead, the Chinese media began to issue some neutral and even positive reports and comments on the United States. However, China was still in the late period of the "Cultural Revolution." Its domestic political turmoil was not over and the country was still not open-minded. The two countries' hostility and isolation for decades had limited the Chinese people's understanding of the United States and promoted stereotypes. Strictly speaking, American studies in China began in the early 1980s. After 20 years of continuous exploration, China's American studies have made great progress and the Chinese people's understanding of the United States has also become more sophisticated.

Recently, on Australia's well-known website show "Asian Boss," there was a video shot in Shanghai — "How do the Chinese feel about the United

States?" — which became popular on the Internet. The authentic views of the United States expressed by ordinary Chinese people triggered a large number of comments from American netizens. Relatively speaking, the Chinese view the United States in a more objective way than previously. In the video, the Chinese people evaluated the United States in an objective way, i.e. based on facts. Generally speaking, their evaluations were very positive[8].

Reporter: How do you feel about the United States? How do you explain your reaction?

Passerby A: I feel it is relatively (a) more free (country). Everyone has good ideas and will share them with others. Its people are more willing to communicate with each other and think in an unrestrained way. What's more, the United States is well developed in entertainment and sports, such as Hollywood, NBA. Its technology is also relatively advanced and everyone likes using iPhones. The shortcoming of the United States is that it is too imperious, which means that the country likes to impose its own ideas on others.

Passerby B: I think the U.S. contribution is indispensable to the world. It plays a leading role in technology, politics, as well as culture.

Reporter: If you have the opportunity to study, work or live in the United States, will you go?

Passerby C: If there is an opportunity, of course I will go. I'd like to travel there.

Passerby D: I think I will not go there. You know the shooting incident that just happened. There seems to be a small flaw in security and order, especially at night, in the United States.

Reporter: Do you think the United States is a safe place?

Passerby E: I think that it is not proper to view the United States as unsafe based only on some shooting incidents. In general, it is a safe place.

Passerby F: U.S. public security is not as good as that in China. In the United States, the racial issue has never been solved, and the country has never shown a united front in solving the gun control issue.

IV. Fading Halo

Today, due to the increasing unilateralism and the bullying behavior reflected in U.S. foreign policy, "disillusionment" with the United States has become a word that has appeared from time to time in political and academic circles, and even in public opinions. China is no exception. The disillusionment is particularly evident among China's elites, who are very familiar with the United States. How does the United States, which was originally "beautiful, free, rational, and progressive," suddenly become so rude and arrogant? The halo of the Statue of Liberty seems to be gradually fading away.

On Independence Day of 2018, the Statue of Liberty was surrounded by chaos. A woman climbed the base of the Statue of Liberty and refused to come down in order to protest the Trump administration's crude immigration policies. Other protesters, with the theme "Lady Liberty is Weeping," unfurled a banner around the base of the statue saying "Abolish ICE (U.S. Immigration and Customs Enforcement)!" At least seven people were arrested on Liberty Island and the site was closed to tourists. Authorities had tried to persuade the woman to come down but she refused. For about two hours, she crossed the base of the statue, at times sitting in the folds of the statue's dress and under Lady Liberty's sandal. Finally, police officers with ropes and climbing devices climbed to the woman. They put ropes and other devices on the woman to bring her down with a ladder.

The woman, identified as Therese Patricia Okoumou, was a member of Rise and Resist, a group of protesters, and had declared that she wouldn't come down until "all the children are released," according to a source with the New York Police Department.

An organizer of Rise and Resist said the theme of the protest was that Lady Liberty is weeping over the unconstitutional excesses of ICE under the Trump administration. "We thought we wanted to do something on our Independence Day, a day that obviously is meant for reflection on the ideals on which this nation was founded. This country has posited itself as a beacon. Right now, we have a government that is actively turning its back on those ideals," said the organizer.

The Trump administration's policy against illegal immigrants, which will cause family separations, had been constantly criticized. Trump eventually made a rare compromise and signed an executive order on June 20, 2018 to withdraw the policy that led to the separation of nearly 2,000 children from their illegal immigrant parents. It's reported that the order also seeks more authority to detain those families together until the end of their immigration proceedings. It's worth noting that according to the New York Times, U.S. health and public service officials said that the 2,000 children who had been separated from their parents could not immediately be reunited with their families. The Guardian quoted CBS journalist Jacqueline Alemany as saying that there would be no "special efforts" made to reunite the children who have been separated from their parents, which means the government will continue to treat them as "unaccompanied" minors.

As early as February 22, 2018, the U.S. Citizenship and Immigration Services (USCIS) suddenly issued a new "Mission Statement." In the new declaration, the bureau deleted the statement "America's promise as a nation of immigrants," but expressed the need to protect the security of Americans and the country as well as respect American values. The publication of the new "Mission Statement" triggered an uproar: the United States has always been a country of immigrants since its inception! Many immigration groups have condemned this change and believe that this goes against the traditional values of the United States.

In the minds of the Chinese public, especially the intellectual elites, what happened under the Statue of Liberty has aggravated their disillusionment with the United States. Wen Xian, the former chief reporter of the *People's Daily* in the United States, published an article titled "Lady Liberty is also an Immigrant." In the article, Wen, who is also an expert on the United States, wrote that "as an immigrant country, the U.S. policy on immigration issues has always been a pendulum. Trump's action is just a piece of U.S. history which has gone from one extreme to the other. The difference is that today, Trump's resolve to go to the extreme is very ironic."

Zhang Jiadong, a professor with the Center for American Studies at Fudan University, wrote that the disillusionment is partly due to the negative effects of the United States as an immigrant society. The immigrant society is an important feature of the United States and one of the roots of this strong nation. Immigrants or their descendants constitute the main part of American scientific research personnel. At present, the United States faces two major changes regarding the immigration issue. First, the immigration structure is changing from one dominated by middle- and high-level talents to one of people from all levels. Moreover, the middle- and low-level immigrants gradually gained the upper hand in the United States, and the number of middle- and high-level talents leaving the United States began to increase. Second, the negative effects of immigration began to be magnified, and social diversification and fragmentation intensified. In order to maintain the dominant position of the white people, the United States adopted the Chinese Exclusion Act, Japanese Exclusion Act, etc., and later adjusted the quantity of immigration through the principle of proportionality.

Wang Jisi, Professor of China's Peking University, said: "I have a strong sense of disillusionment with the United States. When I first went to the United

States in 1984, the political struggle in the country was relatively rational and civilized, different from today when shouting abuse is frequent."

Wang observed that the differentiation of the United States as an immigrant society actually appeared many years ago, but people did not pay much attention to the phenomenon. In 1992, a series of racial riots happened in Los Angeles, not between blacks and whites, but between blacks and Korean immigrants. Now the gaps between different American ethnic groups is gradually deepening, as is the xenophobia.

On the one hand, many blacks and women, who are represented by Barack Obama and Hillary Clinton and have been oppressed, want to establish "political correctness" of multiculturalism; on the other hand, other people hold exactly the opposite opinion and some of them are even openly white supremacists. These two processes occur at the same time. People tend to notice multiculturalism and despise the rebound of right-wing nationalism and racism. In 1991, when he was teaching in the United States, Wang was very cautious not to violate "political correctness" and not to discriminate against blacks and women. In fact, the opposite tendency also existed. For example, a white girl said to Wang privately: "A black girl in the same class is not poorer than me, nor is a work-study student like me, but she enjoys a scholarship. It is unfair!" She found the reverse racial discrimination disgusting. In fact, both blacks and whites feel that they are discriminated against. "The contradiction between the two has not been fully noticed."

Zhang believes that the premise of today's disillusionment with the United States is the previous idealized perception of the country. "In the past, the light of the United States was so dazzling that it hindered people's understanding of its problems and historical facts. " In fact, many of the factors that make people feel disappointed in the United States today have existed since the beginning of the founding of the nation. The United States had established the earliest modern democratic system, while also establishing the last slavery in human history. It, on the one hand, emphasizes human rights and equality, but on the other hand, excludes minorities within the nation; the country appears to champion humanitarianism and universal love, while adopting many bills aimed at excluding foreigners. The United States claims to liberate all mankind and, in fact, has helped many countries and peoples, but at the same time it has expanded and invaded, causing many humanitarian tragedies. But for a long time, out of disappointment with the rest of the world, people are used to imagining the United States, with the Statue of Liberty as its icon, as an ideal country, or even the end of human history. However, the United States is just like any other country.

People feel disillusioned not necessarily because the United States has gone bad, but more likely because the United States has revealed the true face of a sovereign state. The end of the "American Dream" will not be the beginning of the tragedy of human society, but will be a new starting point for development. It is a progress for the international community to create order from disorder. It will be a greater progress at a higher level for the international community to turn from governance by one country to governance by multiple countries. We should remember the positive role the United States played in the cause of human progress and the great contributions it has made, but also its mistakes and even evils. Looking at the country through the perspective of the course of history and giving it an objective assessment are necessary for the future of the United States and the world.

In Boston, Dr. Meng still seeks to reconstruct the "The Empress of China." "I have never given up restoring the 'The Empress of China.' It is a history that deserves to be remembered by both countries. I've made a lot of attempts over the years. Later, I think "resurrection" can be achieved in many ways and aspects, so that everyone is very happy, very conscious to remember it. For example, in 2016, I wrote a historical fantasy novel 'The Original Friendship between the United States and China — the Legend of The Empress of China.' I hope it can be adapted for a globally acknowledged movie with high quality. Let the resurrection of the 'The Empress of China' be first realized in hearts of the global audience."

In her spare time, Dr. Meng will take her daughter for a walk in the backyard and tell her the story of the "The Empress of China." The most important thing, she said, is to show the next generation of the two countries the possibility of cultural fusion, as well as the positive and beautiful prospects following the fusion. "The Empress of China," which was created a century earlier than the Statue of Liberty, is not only about the past, but also about the future.

[1] Jinping Xi, *Speech at a welcoming banquet hosted by the local government of Washington State and American friendly group*. Sept. 22, 2015.

[2] Yangyang Zeng, *The Empress of China: Milestone of American Maritime Silk Road* http://blog.sina.com.cn/s/blog_5ee2829301010kfl.html

[3] Yangyang Zeng, *The Empress of China: Milestone of American Maritime Silk Road* http://blog.sina.com.cn/s/blog_5ee2829301010kfl.html

[4] Yangyang Zeng, *The Empress of China: Milestone of American Maritime Silk Road* http://blog.sina.com.cn/s/blog_5ee2829301010kfl.html

[5] Thomas M. Paine, *Connected: Tracing back to China* /6 NOV 2015/; http://citieswithheart.com/the-boston-guangzhou-connection-cctv-comes-to-pem/

[6] Xianzhang Zhang, *Fantasies on Statue of Liberty*, Popular Tribune. 2004,01. http://kns.cnki.net/KCMS/detail/detail.aspx?dbcode=CJFQ&dbname=CJFD2004&filename=QYYT200401012&v=MTQ1NDBlWDFMdXhZUzdEaDFUM3FUcldNMUZyQ1VSTEtlWnVSdkZpRGdWN3JBTkRUU2VyRzRIdFhNcm85RVpvUjg=

[7] Mei Zhao, *America's Image in Chinese High School History Textbooks:A Survey since the Late Qing Dynasty*, The Chinese Journal of American Studies. 2006,04. http://www.cnki.com.cn/Article/CJFDTotal-MGYJ200604002.htm

[8] Asian Boss: *This is How The Chinese See America* https://v.youku.com/v_show/id_XMzY4MjEwMDczNg==.html

[9] Xian Wen, *The Statue of Liberty is immigrant*. Global People, 2018, 14. http://

www.fx361.com/page/2018/0804/3969583.shtml
[10] Jiadong Zhang, *Why there is a sense of disillusionment with U.S. today*. https://baijiahao.baidu.com/s?id=1615246125023015311&wfr=spider&for=pc
[11] Wang Jisi: *Leaving China is not the reason why the United States launches Trade War, FT(Chinese)* http://www.ftchinese.com/story/001079777?archive

Chapter Six

Fake News and Real Gaps

"If all you have is a hammer, everything looks like a nail."

— Bernard Baruch

CNN = FNN!?

U.S. President Donald Trump posted a spoof video on his Twitter account on July 2, 2017, replacing the logo of CNN (Cable News Network) with FNN (Fraud News Network) at the end of the footage.[1] Since the election of Trump, who doesn't follow the norm and often dismisses news stories or media outlets that he doesn't like as "fake news," the phrase "fake news" has spread like wildfire.

Trump berated CNN reporter Jim Acosta when he asked the president about his stance against a U.S.-bound migrant caravan from Central America at a White House press conference on November 7, 2018.

"When you report fake news, which CNN does a lot, you are the enemy of the people," Trump told Acosta during a heated exchange with the CNN reporter.[2]

It's an unprecedented phenomenon for the U.S. president to "govern the country via Twitter." The tensions between Trump and a number of influential U.S. media outlets are unprecedented as well. In a modern society featuring web-based social media that enable people to be online at any time, Trump's concept of "fake news" has blurred or even overturned the definition within the context of traditional ethics of journalism.

A more worrying scenario is that, when the concept was used to define international relations with a double standard, such as Sino-U.S. ties, it will further deepen misunderstanding between countries, thus making bilateral relations, which have always had "an information gap," more complicated.

I. The Easy Scapegoat

"Regrettably, we found that China has been attempting to interfere in our upcoming 2018 election coming up in November against my administration," Trump said at the UN Security Council on September 26, 2018.[3]

"They do not want me or us to win because I am the first president ever to challenge China on trade," Trump said during a session meant to focus on issues of nonproliferation of weapons of mass destruction and their means of delivery, diverging from the topic of the meeting.

The following arrangements indicated that it might not have been an off-the-cuff remark by Trump. Trump and White House officials on the same day revealed time and again the astonishing "fact" at several occasions and by different means, such as via tweets, at a press conference, during a meeting with Japanese Prime Minister Shinzo Abe, and at a telephone briefing to the media.

TV footage shows that Chinese State Councilor and Foreign Minister Wang Yi, who was attending the UN Security Council meeting, shook his head and shrugged his shoulders when he heard Trump's remarks. He is not the only one who wanted to do that. Even some U.S. congressmen and experts on information safety felt confused to hear Trump's outrageous statements.

Maybe due to the vagueness of Trump's remarks which are counter-intuitive, the makers of "fake news" — U.S. mainstream media — can only guess why Trump made these statements, blaming China at such a high-level international event. They guess Trump intended to divert the public's attention from a number of negative news reports, such as the sexual assault allegation against a federal judge nominee and judicial trials against some members of Trump's presidential campaign team, or that he was worrying about the Republicans in the 2018 midterm elections.

Following the midterm election, the Democratic Party won back the House of Representatives while the Republicans remained in control of the Senate. Both Trump and the Democrats claimed victory respectively in the election. However, by the end of the midterm election, the White House had offered no concrete evidence to back up its allegation against China.

Giving few details on how China had been attempting to interfere in the election, the only name the White House mentioned is an English-language newspaper from China — *China Daily*.

The accusation against *China Daily* is that it published advertisements which explained to the U.S. readers the economic costs of the China-U.S. trade disputes, in the *Des Moines Register* newspaper.

It conforms to U.S. law and is a very common practice for foreign media to publish advertisements in U.S. newspapers such as the *Washington Post* and the *New York Times*. *China Daily* was qualified to publish paid-ads years ago.

The U.S. president and his aides and staff should be quite familiar with K Street, which links the White House and the Capitol in Washington D.C. It's well known for hosting a large number of think tanks, NGO headquarters, lobby groups and public relations corporations.

Compared with what happened on this street, what the Chinese newspaper did is just to record truthfully some U.S. citizens' opinions against Trump's protectionist policies on trade. Even some U.S. media were surprised to see the Chinese newspaper being labeled as a meddler "interfering in the U.S. election" by Trump.

II. The Innocent Christmas Tree

"Three, two, one!" — Following the audience's countdown at the National Mall in downtown Washington, D.C. on the afternoon of November 30, 2012, a series of explosions broke out with thick black smoke rising above a 13-meter-high pine tree. Five seconds of silence followed, but were soon broken by a second explosion that lasted for another few seconds. Fireworks were set off from the tree, creating a scene that resembled the traditional lighting up of a Christmas tree in the United States. While the smoke had just dissipated, a third big explosion occurred instantly, soon after which thick black smoke once again emerged from atop the Christmas tree. The piece of artwork featuring exploding gunpowder by Chinese artist Cai Guo-qiang was thus completed.

Cai said the work was merely another episode of his "black explosion" series. As Christmas was nearing, people from New York where Cai lived and Washington where his work was displayed had been elaborately decorating their Christmas trees. Unlike the commonly seen illuminated Christmas trees at night, Cai, in his uniqueness, presented a "Christmas tree in the daytime" and highlighted the contrast via black explosions. When the last trace of black smoke vanished from the top of the tree, the effects created were those similar to a Chinese ink painting, namely ink soaking and spreading on the paper. A free-flowing ink painting of a pine tree was thus recreated. Cai felt the ongoing sluggish economy had affected the lives as well as the moods of many people during the holiday season. The "black Christmas tree," he said, showcased a sense of "black humor" that resonated with reality.

"Washington is such a serious place and it's good to try something relaxing and amusing," Cai said with a smile.[4]

The unique work of art was recognized by many in the United States, including the then U.S. Secretary of State Hillary Clinton. Even while showcasing discontent with reality, the artist's black sense of humor was met with laughter as well as applause from most of the audience.

However, the Chinese artist who has lived in Japan and the United States for many years and traveled all around the world might not know that his work has been given "black metaphoric meanings" by Michael Pillsbury, an American scholar who claims to be a China expert.

In his bestseller *The Hundred-Year Marathon*, Pillsbury, using details, seeks to remind Americans: Think about this, a Chinese has "exploded" a "Christmas tree" which symbolizes Christian culture at the heart of the capital of the world's only superpower. This is just going too far!

Pillsbury might not know that Cai and his works have gained even greater popularity and reputation in China just for his international background and the vision, artistry and humor it has thus nurtured.

Cai has become recognized for his performance art of gunpowder blasting. His most familiar works to Chinese include "extending the Great Wall with an extra distance of 10,000 meters," which was displayed in the Gobi desert outside the Jiayu Pass of the Great Wall in 1993, and the 29 "big footprints" created by fireworks at the opening ceremony of the 2008 Beijing Olympic Games. If the Chinese were to interpret Cai's art the way Pillsbury did, they might only be more justified in feeling offended, given what Cai has "exploded" is an ancient defense project the whole nation takes pride in and what he has "trodden" upon with all eyes on is China's capital city.

Most Chinese on the scene would have known that black humor is an "imported" aesthetic variety for China and it might just happen to be from the

United States. Why, in this sense, would Cai's use of it in his "black Christmas tree"elicit questions?

About *The Hundred-Year Marathon*, a more well-known American scholar, Charles Freeman, has candidly said, "I think the book you refer to is nonsensical conspiracy theory. It is not taken seriously as scholarship by anyone of note in the China field. It is widely seen by experts as a polemic, in which there are multiple distortions of both facts and sources. It is, unfortunately, far from the only polemical work on China to have gained a significant readership."

"It means that the United States can no longer claim superiority in some arenas or act unilaterally but must recognize the emergence not only of China, but of other power centers. These are facts and trends, not the product of some sort of Chinese plot," said Freeman, who was the main interpreter when then U.S. President Richard Nixon visited China in 1972.

III. Still Softer than Soft

"If someone puts a gun to your head and demands your wallet, it does not matter what you want or think. That is hard power. If that person is trying to persuade you to freely give up your wallet, everything depends on what you want or think. That is soft power."

Joseph Nye, the well-known Harvard scholar who proposed the concept of "soft power," vividly said so in a Foreign Affairs article. He reiterated that soft power is the ability to affect others by attraction and persuasion, whereas hard power is based on coercion and payment.[5]

As a leader of the international order after World War II and the only remaining superpower after the Cold War, the United States has never been short of "strategists." Many of them have dealt with China a lot and some have even earned the distinction of being "China hands." In the past year or so, a group of think tanks, the academic community and media in the United States and Europe have once again discredited China's efforts to boost its global image and influence. The concept they have coined this time is "sharp power".

In fact, though China has always been regarded as "inspired" by the soft power theory, its intent has never been to "put a gun to your head and demand your wallet" or to persuade others to "freely give up your wallet." What China intends to do is to have itself heard and recognized by more people worldwide, thereby improving its global image that has long been questioned and even smeared, and sharing with the world its own experiences so that other countries, too, may benefit.

As one can imagine, in an increasingly "flat" world, how would a man who has just survived the trauma of war and the plight of hunger and received some hard-won money willingly be always called a "sick man," an "upstart" and a "dictator"? The problem is, however, that his expressions of ideas may not be proficient enough and are too easy to be taken out of context in a system of discourse dominated by the West. When resorting to his own discourse system, he may become the target of attacks.

Western "referees," with a sense of superiority and experienced in attacking opponents with an iron fist in a velvet glove during the Cold War, firmly believe that China's development of its soft power must have also been driven by the ulterior motive of a zero-sum game. They have even redefined China's regular public diplomacy and foreign exchanges as "sharp power".

In Joseph Nye's opinion, the dividing line between "soft power" and "sharp power" lies in "truth and openness." When China's state news agency reports openly in other countries, it is employing soft power, which should be accepted, said Nye. In fact, the criterion to draw the distinction is dependent on the fairness of the "referees." For instance, President Trump and the CNN reporter with whom he got into a fight at the White House press conference on November 7 must have had different understandings of "fake news".

When it comes to the term of power, those accustomed to a zero-sum mentality may immediately associate it with competition and overlook its connotation of "strength" in the first place. Strength can be mobilized for confrontation, but more so for cooperation.

"I don't think China's soft power can compete with the United States globally in the short term," said Kenneth Jarrett, president of the American Chamber of Commerce in Shanghai, in a speech delivered in Beijing in the summer of 2018.

Nye has been candid about the positive effects soft power may bring. He said, when giving an example, that if both China and the United States want to refrain from conflicts, the enhancement of exchange projects that appeal to both sides will be mutually beneficial. Soft power can also help boost mutual trust between the two countries and make possible the resolving of transnational issues such as climate change via cooperation.

Freeman believes that China's efforts to express itself and introduce its achievements to the world are not excessive. "The Chinese model is uniquely Chinese. I don't believe it can be exported. Nor do I see China attempting to export it. I know of no people who seek to emulate China's current political system, though many admire China's socioeconomic achievements and scientific progress. Some Americans, including politicians, may object to public diplomacy by China, but I believe most welcome the opportunity to learn more about China and its views."

To express itself properly and not be misunderstood: There is nothing complex in China's efforts to boost its soft power.

But the reality is that far from too many, there have been too few occasions that China has been able to express itself clearly, too few Chinese who can express themselves to the world effectively and too little development of China's "soft power." Up to today, misinterpretations and misunderstandings of China persist.

IV. An Imagined Chinese Dish

"General Tso's Chicken," sometimes called "Zuo Zongtang Chicken" or "Zuo Gong Ji," is a popular dish served in Chinese restaurants in the United States. The sweet and spicy chicken dish was named after Zuo Zongtang, a Qing dynasty statesman and military leader from Hunan Province.

"The Search for General Tso", a documentary that premiered in 2014, explores the secret of the famous dish. American filmmakers found that General Tso, in fact, has nothing to do with the dish, which appeared in Taiwan nearly 70 years after the death of the 19th-century general. It was invented by Peng Chang-kuei, a Hunanese chef to former Kuomintang leader Chiang Kai-shek.[6]

"General Tso's Chicken" enjoyed growing popularity across the United States as more Chinese restaurants opened following former President Nixon's visit to China in 1972. The dish also reportedly became a favorite of famed scholar and diplomat Henry Kissinger and was highly-rated by The New York Times. Now it has become a specialty on the menu of Chinese restaurants in the United States.

However, the popular dish in the United States is not likely to be found in China, as its average sweet-and-sour flavor will not likely appeal to the taste buds of Chinese foodies. It's also hard to imagine that any restaurant in China would serve so-called "Chinese cuisine" imported from North America. If anyone tries to know and understand authentic Chinese cuisine through "General Tso's Chicken," they are obviously wrong and will miss the rich culture and profound history behind it.

Since the end of World War II, Western cultures, especially American culture, have prevailed and influenced the world. Its impact on China is no exception. China has always adopted an open attitude toward cultural exchanges between China and the West. "The Wonderful Read", a book-reading show started in October 2018, has become one of the most popular variety shows on the Internet in China. It recommended good books to Chinese audiences, especially young readers, in the form of drama performances and academic analysis.

Among the recommended bibliographies were Western literary classics like *The Moon and Sixpence* and *Love in the Time of Cholera*, as well as books by Chinese writers including award-winning science fiction *The Three-Body Problem* by Liu Cixin, who says frankly that he has been greatly inspired by Western masters of science fiction, and *1587, A Year of No Significance: The Ming Dynasty in Decline* by historian Ray Huang, a Chinese American scholar who once worked at Columbia University and Harvard.

America's influence on pop culture is profound. Hollywood is now focusing more on China's vast film market. According to the 2017 Chinese Residents' Consumption Development Report by the National Development and Reform Commission of China, the total box office of Chinese films in 2012 was only 25 percent of that of the North American market, and in 2017 it reached 77.63 percent.[7] The box office of Hollywood blockbusters in China repeatedly surpassed their North American box office counterparts, becoming a main promoter of the global box office. For example, data suggest that "xXx: Return of Xander Cage" grossed 346 million U.S. dollars at the global box office, to which the Chinese mainland contributed 170 million U.S. dollars, or as much as 49 percent. In stark contrast, its North American box office was only 44.89 million U.S. dollars, or 13 percent of its global revenue. On the other hand, Chinese films, even popular and critically acclaimed productions, either cannot enter U.S. mainstream theaters or have a very poor box office performance.

American dramas are the top choice for many young Chinese. Although Chinese original online dramas enjoy growing popularity, their overseas influence is far dwarfed by American dramas. In 2017, the Chinese online detective drama "Day and Night" received 4 billion views in China and a score of 9 out of 10 from nearly 250,000 users of China's film review site Douban. Netflix acquired the hit drama's overseas copyright at the end of 2017. By November 2018, only 464 users of U.S. movies database site IMDb rated the drama. However, a similar American crime drama, "True Detective: Season 1," has been rated by more than 70,000 Chinese users on Douban.

In today's world where Western mainstream culture forms the center of the world culture, Chinese stories have yet to be sufficiently narrated, nor has the "voice" of China and the ancient oriental culture been properly heard. Behind the trust deficit between China and the United States is "information inequality." In other words, China knows much more about America than America knows about China.

V. Arabella's Gift

By reciting Tang poetry and the Three-Character Classic and singing Chinese children's songs, talented six-year-old Arabella Rose Kushner, granddaughter of U.S. President Trump, suddenly attracted global attention.

In November 2017, Trump showed Chinese President Xi Jinping a video of his granddaughter Arabella Kushner singing in Mandarin and reciting ancient Chinese poems. Her wonderful performance left a deep impression on the Chinese people.[8]

If there are political implications that the First Family of the United States let their children learn Chinese, "Chinese fever" among young people around the world is definitely their spontaneous choice. Whatever the political implications of the First Family of the United States letting their children learn Chinese, Chinese is indeed becoming increasingly popular among young people around the world.

American financial tycoon Jim Rogers also showed people videos of his two daughters speaking fluent and accent-free Mandarin. Amazon founder Jeff Bezos and Facebook CEO Mark Zuckerberg have made it clear that they want their children to learn Chinese.

"I had the feeling China was the future," George H.W. Bush, the 41st President of the United States, said in an interview as he explained why he decided to accept the role as chief of the U.S. Liaison Office to China in 1974 instead of other positions in the U.K. and France.

Bush thought the U.S. approach to the Soviet Union would not work for China. Instead of confronting it, it is better to learn from each other more and reduce differences.

According to a Gallup poll released on June 6, 2013, as much as 72 percent of Americans between the ages of 18 and 29 saw China as a friend or even an ally of the United States.[9]

The American public's views toward China vary from generation to generation. The reason may be that the younger generation is growing up in a more multipolar world. As the world is becoming smaller due to the advancement of communications technology, Chinese schoolmates, Chinese cuisine, Made-in-China products, "Kung Fu Panda" and real pandas in zoos all seem closer for the younger generation.

The number of American students studying Mandarin in primary and secondary schools doubled from 2009 to 2015, and the figure will keep growing, according to a survey conducted by American Councils for International Education in June 2017. The survey also showed that Mandarin ranked the fourth most widely taught foreign language in the country's education system.[10]

Rogers made the decision to have his two daughters learn Mandarin because he has long believed that the 21st century is the so-called century of China. To make the next generation better integrate into the new century, they have to learn Mandarin.

The young Americans who are working hard to learn Mandarin may not grow up to bargain with China at the negotiating table or become U.S. foreign policymakers or experts on China. Perhaps, it seems more important for them to be able to cook one or two Chinese dishes, sing Chinese songs and say "Ni Hao" ("How are you doing?") to their Chinese peers on the other side of the Pacific.

In 2012, former U.S. diplomat Charles W. "Chas" Freeman Jr. published a book titled *Interesting Times: China, America and the Shifting Balance of Prestige* on the occasion of the 40th anniversary of Nixon's visit to China.

How to understand and translate "interesting" in the title, the word even most Chinese primary school students can read? You may list a dozen Chinese translations for the word, but Freeman is more inclined to translate it into "troubled times," namely a challenging period of endless emergencies, which still applies to the current China-U.S. relations.[11]

In the process of China-U.S. exchanges, difficulties in translation often come from misunderstandings and lack of communication. These inherent or man-made problems are hard to avoid as the two countries have huge differences in history, society and culture. Perhaps the young generation will have more wisdom to solve them.

[1] *New York Times*, July 2 2017, https://www.nytimes.com/2017/07/02/business/media/trump-wrestling-video-cnn-twitter.html

[2] Washington Post, November 7 2018 *Trump berates CNN's Jim Acosta in contentious White House news conference*, https://www.washingtontimes.com/news/2018/nov/7/donald-trump-berates-jim-acosta-contentious-white-/

[3] CNN, September 28 2018 *Trump says China is interfering in midterm elections*, https://edition.cnn.com/2018/09/26/politics/china-midterms-donald-trump/index.html

[4] Xinhua News Agency, Chinese artist's gunpowder show stuns Washington Dec.1, 2012 http://news.cri.cn/gb/36724/2012/12/03/6471s3945840.htm

[5] Foreign Affairs, February 5 2018 *How Sharp Power Threatens Soft Power* https://www.foreignaffairs.com/articles/china/2018-01-24/how-sharp-power-threatens-soft-power

[6] The Search for General Tso 2014, Director Ian Cheney.

[7] 2017 Report on Development of Chinese consumer spending, People's Publishing House.

[8] Washington Post, November 9 2017, *Trump's granddaughter gets praise and sympathy for singing for Chinese president* https://www.washingtonpost.com/news/worldviews/wp/2017/11/09/trumps-granddaughter-gets-praise-and-sympathy-for-singing-for-chinese-president/?noredirect=on&utm_term=.bf469d84f7bb

[9] Gallup, June 6, 2013, In U.S., More See China as Friend than Foe, https://news.gallup.com/poll/162935/u.s.-more-see-china-friend-foe.aspx

[10] American Councils for International Education 2017 June The National K-12 Foreign Language Enrollment Survey Report https://www.americancouncils.org/sites/default/files/FLE-report-June17.pdf

[11] Sun Hao: "China-U.S. relations in 'troubled time': Fu Limin", *China Financial Weekly*.

Chapter Seven

Aircraft Carriers and the Great Wall

I think that you would have to conclude that this is a great wall and that it had to be built by a great people.

— Richard Nixon, 1972

On an early spring day in 1984, U.S. President Ronald Reagan and his wife Nancy climbed the Great Wall during their first visit to China. Standing on the magnificent ancient military facility, Reagan said China and the Great Wall were in a sense alike, both "impressive and profound".

While President Reagan was giving his compliments, another kind of magnificent military facility — state-of-the-art and all American — was actually not far from where he stood. Aircraft carriers from the U.S. Navy's Seventh Fleet were cruising in the West Pacific waters, close to the Chinese mainland but thousands of miles away from the contiguous United States.

Aircraft carriers and the Great Wall were both built for military purposes but they represent two very different types of thinking in military philosophy.

Stretching over 6,000 kilometers, the Great Wall, a defensive facility that has been standing in north China for more than 2,000 years, speaks of a defensive mindset deeply imbedded in the Chinese culture. Military facilities are for defense — that is how an ordinary Chinese looks at his country's army. The Chinese even call, with pride, the country's navy "the Great Wall at Sea" because it is for defending China's waters just as what the Great Wall did for the country's land. This defensive facility has become one of China's greatest prides as well as one of its most famous cultural symbols. Even Chinese basketball players in the NBA, like Yao Ming and Wang Zhizhi, were often called "the Moving Great Wall" by their fans.

About two decades after Reagan's visit to the Great Wall, a new, 100,000-ton aircraft carrier named after him joined the Seventh Fleet as the world's largest carrier at the time. In recent years, the USS Ronald Reagan has participated in many U.S. military operations in the South China Sea.

I. To Build a Wall to Prevent a War: a Story on Peace for 2,000 Years

Six U.S. presidents, including Ronald Reagan, have so far visited the Great Wall. They were all quite generous with compliments on the miracle created by the ancient Chinese and, obviously, "great" was the word they most frequently used. However, the true greatness of the Great Wall probably cannot be fully understood by merely one visit.

On an autumn night in 2014, President Xi Jinping and President Barack Obama strolled side by side at Yingtai, Zhongnanhai, enjoying the calm scenery and tasting tea. Zhongnanhai serves as the central headquarters for the Communist Party of China and the State Council of China. It is the very center of China's politics and has witnessed many historic events over the past century. During their "white-shirt-and-no-tie" meeting, Xi told his U.S. guest that the Great Wall was a symbol of the Chinese people's pursuit of peace; there are no "genes of expansion" in the Chinese culture, and the great rejuvenation of the Chinese nation means only to achieve great self-development.

The Great Wall has always been a means of defense against invasion by the nomads from the north since the beginning of its construction more than 20 centuries ago. It was completed after generations of sweat, tears and hardship. For most of the time in history, the high walls served as a barrier against the nomadic cavalries invading the fertile southern plains.

However, the success of the Great Wall is not the reason behind the Chinese people's preference to a defensive approach to military policies. In fact, it was the other way around. It was the peace-loving nature of the Chinese people that prompted them to come up with the idea of "building a wall to prevent a war."

In his *Philosophy of History*, G. W. F. Hegel said that "the true theatre of History is ... the temperate zone; or, rather, its northern half." Unique natural conditions, in addition to the cultures of self-sufficiency of the agrarian civilization, have produced the typically "continental" personality of the Chinese nation, lacking internal drives for expansion. The core area of Chinese civilization is seated in a geographically enclosed place where it faces the Pacific Ocean in the east, and mountains and deserts in the other three directions, which has bred a conservative and introverted culture.

The fierce war between Athens and Sparta around 2,500 years ago has been an important subject not only for scholars studying history but also those studying international relations and wars. In particular, realists in the West, inspired by *History of the Peloponnesian War*, a masterpiece by ancient Greek historian Thucydides, have claimed that a rising power will inevitably pose a threat to the established power and lead to war. This also gave rise to the prediction of an "inevitable war" between China and the United States.

The first construction of the Great Wall coincided with the time of the

Peloponnesian War. During that time, China was also at war, centuries of war. It was called the times of "Spring and Autumn" and the "Warring States". But Chinese philosophers drew a different conclusion from it: Confucius chose "Ren" (which means "humaneness", "goodness", "benevolence" or "love" in Chinese) as the core of his philosophy and criticized military conquests for being not in line with the principles of "Ren". Mo Tzu, whose fundamental doctrine is undifferentiated love (Jianai), regarded wars as ominous and disastrous. Laozi also believed that war was an "ominous device" and should be used only as a last resort. Despite their profound differences in political beliefs, the pre-Qin philosophers all agreed on opposing wars.

Among all the pre-Qin philosophers, the military strategists have drawn the most attention of Western scholars but are also one of the most misunderstood groups. Scholars in the West more often than not believe that the ancient military strategists were warmongers. But they hardly were. Sunzi, whose masterpiece *The Art of War* is often hailed as the "Bible of wars", actually was a pacifist. In his famous book, the greatest military strategist in ancient Chinese history clearly concluded that a first-class military strategist wins wars by outmaneuvering his enemies; a second-class strategist wins wars by sabotaging relations between his enemies; a third-class strategist wins wars by defeating his enemies' army on the battlefield; and a worst strategist would siege his enemies' cities. In principle, Sunzi believed strategic and diplomatic maneuvers are much better options than the use of force. Wu Qi, another military strategist in ancient China, also had a famous teaching that "one's failure is inevitable after going through five wars," which warns that indulging in the use of military might will inevitably lead to one's own downfall. This notion of "be the mighty but do not abuse your might" is also reflected in Kung Fu, another symbol of Chinese culture. In an action movie of Bruce Lee or Jackie Chan, the hero should not only excel at martial arts but also has to be morally irreproachable. The true meaning of Kung Fu lies in physical fitness, defense and not being a bully.

The ideology of "He" (which means harmony and peace in Chinese) has had immense influence over China's diplomatic practices throughout history. Even nowadays, epigrams like "A harmonious family can prosper in every aspect" are still popular among the Chinese. Ancient Chinese emperors usually favoured the use of diplomatic means to deal with conflicts with other countries. One of the many pacifying policies they used was "He-qin", which means marrying Chinese princesses to rulers of minority nationalities in the border areas so as to make peace. The "He-qin" policy bonded together the central empire and minority tribes in the border areas; everyone is in one big family now so there is no need to fight.

In the 15th century, when the Ming Dynasty was still in its early bright, the world's largest and most advanced ships by far at that time were built by the Chinese. With a displacement of 800 tons, such a ship could accommodate more than 1,000 people. Zheng He, the leader of the world's largest fleet at that time, was different from his contemporary navigators. At the order of Emperor Yongle, Zheng led the enormous fleet to the oceans seven times, sailing to Southeast Asia, the Arabian Peninsula and eventually the east coast of Africa. Zheng had an entourage of more than 10,000 people — veteran sailors, well-trained soldiers and merchants — which gave him the capability to colonize any place he visited. But unlike Vasco da Gama, Christopher Columbus or Ferdinand Magellan, Zheng He never attempted to establish a Chinese colony but returned to China after carrying out his mission.

Western historians argued that if Ming China did not stop its overseas expeditions, the Portuguese colonizers would find it difficult to establish their footholds on the Indian coasts and might score little in Malacca, Sumatra and Siam. However, the assumption is derived by typical Western thinking and has zero possibility of realization in China, a country with a long tradition of peace. The Ming Dynasty also had a "tributary system" that Westerners are interested in. James Mattis, defense secretary of the Trump Administration, has on many public occasions claimed China is trying to control their neighbors and reestablish the tributary system. The tributary system in ancient China was complicated; to better understand it, one could refer to the introduction in *The Cambridge History of China.*

Citing the example of China-Korea relations in the Ming Dynasty, the book gives a detailed account of the tributary system from which one may realize the mistakes Secretary Mattis has made. The tributary system has four characteristics:

First, China always returned more to the tribute-offering countries. Not only did the Ming court give the Korean envoys of tributes high-profile receptions, it also gave back more expensive gifts. Sometimes the Ministry of Rites would even protest because the Korean envoys came to pay tribute too often, costing the treasury too much money.

Second, the tributary system was an important part of China-Korea trade. The envoys would carry goods along their journey to Beijing and privately trade them with Chinese merchants. The great opportunity to make profits was at least part of the reason why Koreans were keen to visit China.

Third, it promoted cultural communication between China and Korea. Books from China may be the items that had exerted the most far-reaching impact on the Korean Peninsula. The code of the earlier Ming Dynasty was the model for the Koreans when they made their first code in 1394. The tributary system served as a channel of incomparable importance in terms of cultural communication between the two nations.

Fourth, the tributary system provided Korea with security insurance. At the end of the 16th century, Toyotomi Hideyoshi launched two wars of aggression against Korea after he had unified Japan. The Ming Dynasty spared no effort and no cost to aid the Koreans in defending their country. Toyotomi's attempt to conquer the Korean Peninsula was foiled, with Ming China paying a hefty price. During the first Japanese invasion alone, China had to mobilize about 200,000 soldiers and spend as much as 10 million liangs (or tael, the traditional Chinese weight unit, which equals about 37.5 grams) of silver. On the basis of purchasing power, this was worth about 10 billion U.S. dollars and accounted for nearly half of the Ming Dynasty's annual fiscal revenue. Some long-standing characteristics of China's foreign policies were included in the Ming Dynasty's tributary system, scholars concluded in *The Cambridge History of China*, saying that ancient China's foreign policies in general were "defensive" and characterized by restraint in international affairs.

"What's past is prologue." Throughout its history, China has no record of aggression or expansion against foreign nations. The Great Wall, which has stood for thousands of years, witnessed and will continue to witness China's practice of defensive military strategies. Having studied all 11 wars and conflicts in which China was involved from 1840 to 1980, U.S. political scientist Jonathan Adelman found that China's purpose of using force was different from that of the West; the primary goal of a war was not to acquire territory, defeat the enemy or gain power but to show determination, embarrass or punish the enemy, and self-defend, which is entirely traditional Chinese thinking on wars.

Despite the lack of any substantial evidence either in history or reality, the unfounded imagination of "China threats" has been easy to sell. It might be helpful going over a popular ancient fable in China about a man in the country of Qi constantly worrying that the sky would collapse and fall down. One day, a wise man explained to him what the sky and earth were composed of, and the man finally let go of his misgivings and felt great relief. Instead of worrying about the imaginary "China threats", the proponents of such claims should get rid of the prejudices and try to understand the real China.

First of all, China's actual defense investment and military capability are often exaggerated. Overemphasizing China's total military spending and its global ranking without due context can often cause people to neglect both China's enormous economy and population. As a matter of fact, China's military expenditure as a share of GDP and the country's per capita military expenditure are both lower than those of other world powers. In the past 10 years, China's military expenditure accounted for on average only 1.32 percent of its GDP, not only far below the 4 percent of the United States, Russia and other major world powers but also much lower than the world average of 2.4 percent. In 2016, for instance, China's military expenditure was equivalent to only 24.6 percent of that of the United States. The ratio per thousand inhabitants of active military was only 13.58 percent of that of the United States, 34.4 percent of that of Japan and 22.98 percent of that of Britain.

Pierre Picard, who has a PhD in geopolitics from the University of Paris 8, said in 2015 that in recent years a significant part of the increase in China's military spending had gone to programs aimed at improving the working and living conditions of soldiers. The increase was also partly offset by inflation, as is the opinion of Edward Schwark, a research fellow at the London-based Royal United Services Institute, who argues that the impact of inflation should not be ignored and that there actually has not been such a big increase in China's military spending.

Bonnie Glaser, a senior adviser for Asia in the Freeman Chair in China Studies at the Center for Strategic and International Studies, published an article "5 Common Myths About China's Power" in 2016, in which she referred her point, "China is a global military superpower," to the first myth.

"Superpowers must project power globally, but China's capabilities remain bounded to East Asia," she wrote.

Second, China's efforts in increasing its military capability can largely be characterized as "repairing the Great Wall". The world's largest developing nation has in the past 30 years been focusing on developing its economy, while its defense capability has not kept pace. In this sense, China's defense capability has been somewhat lagging behind other major world powers. Neither has it been commensurate with China's economic development.

In 2008, China's military expenditure rose to be No. 2 in the world for the first time, a development that was greeted with skepticism. Nevertheless, analyses done by some think tanks shed light on the development. A 2009 article published on Spanish website Observatorio de Politica China pointed out that the increase in China's military expenditure largely reflected an attempt to make up for what has been left behind in terms of defense. China, said the article, was seriously outdated in terms of its military equipment compared with the developed countries or even some of its neighbors. Tanks deployed in the Chinese army, for instance, were mainly those outdated models taking after the designs of the former Soviet Union. China made 80 percent of its military aircraft but their designs were largely based on warplanes that used to (be?) the Soviet mainstream decades ago. Meanwhile, in China's neighborhood, the Republic of Korea was speeding up the process of updating its military equipment by deploying the K-2 tank, anti-tank fighters and F-15K jets. Japan was producing F-2 fighters with a price tag of over 100 million U.S. dollars per jet and was able to make the TK-X, said to be the world's most advanced and most expensive tank.

Third, the increase in China's military expenditure was essential for protecting its own security even with its defensive stance. Li Mingjiang, an associate professor at the S. Rajaratnam School of International Studies, Nanyang Technological University, said that, from a long-term perspective, there is a significant gap between China's military capability and the realistic needs to ensure its defense security, modernize its military and protect its national interests. China faces a multitude of security challenges, perhaps more than any other major world power, especially in the Asia-Pacific region.

Overseas security, or protection of its interests overseas, has also come to be increasingly important for China with the deepening of its reform and opening-up. Statistics show that residents of the Chinese mainland made 146 million overseas trips in 2017. The number of Chinese-invested enterprises in other countries and regions had risen to more than 30,000, while Chinese nationals working abroad numbered about 1 million and Chinese students studying overseas numbered 1.37 million. In 2017 alone, 126 Chinese nationals died in other countries in incidents of security and 102 Chinese workers were killed in safety incidents while on duty. These deaths were most reported in Southeast Asia and places in Central Asia, West Asia and North Africa where Chinese companies were often undertaking construction projects. Security protection thus has emerged as an essential need along the Belt and Road, a development initiative aimed at boosting development potentials by providing the necessary infrastructural links both on land and sea from Asia through Africa to Europe and even Latin America.

This need for security guarantee to keep up with economic activities resonates with the functions of the Great Wall in history. In the Qin Dynasty some 2,000 years ago, the 12 prefectures along the Great Wall were connected by mainroads to facilitate the delivery of mails and the commerce and travels. In the Han Dynasty, the main roads were further extended west, with the Great

Wall as part of the security guarantee for commerce along the Silk Road. In a sense, nowadays China's "Maritime Great Wall" is a means of providing essential security for commerce along the 21st century Maritime Silk Road. The Chinese Navy has been conducting escort missions in the Gulf of Aden and waters off Somali to fend off pirates for 10 consecutive years, providing for the critical safety needs of more than 6,000 Chinese and foreign ships.

Fourth, China's participation in missions aimed at safeguarding regional and world peace says a lot about its intentions. Actions speak. China's armed forces have never been involved in invasions of foreign countries but have, instead, participated in more and more peacekeeping missions. China was one of the key contributors to peacekeeping missions highlighted in a series of pictures and videos made by the United Nations in May 2018 to show its appreciation for the efforts of the participating countries. One of the videos featured the Chinese peacekeeping infantry battalion in South Sudan, with two distinctive red lanterns outside the door of the camp and a motto in Chinese characters in couplet style meaning "LOYALLY FULFILL MISSIONS" and "SAFEGUARD WORLD PEACE". Such pledges have been honored by the Chinese peacekeepers, which often has to be done at the cost of the lives of their soldiers. Two years ago, two young Chinese soldiers were killed and five others wounded in Juba when a peacekeeping vehicle was hit by a rocket in a fierce clash between armed factions of the South Sudanese forces. The soldiers were there because the Chinese infantry battalion had been charged with protecting the No.1 IDP camp that was exposed to the crossfire. China has dispatched 37,000 peacekeepers, more than any other country in the world, to participate in 24 UN peacekeeping missions over the past 28 years since it first participated in such missions. China has also been the second largest contributor of funds to the UN peacekeeping missions over these years.

China and its neighbors have had expanding cooperation in recent years in safeguarding regional peace and stability. It has been working together with several neighbors in combating terrorism-related human smuggling, arresting a number of terrorist suspects and human smugglers. These efforts dealt a heavy blow to the illegal human smuggling networks, and effectively countered and prevented the infiltration of terrorist organizations.

China has been active in disaster relief cooperation in the Asia-Pacific, providing aid to countries such as Malaysia, Myanmar and Sri Lanka.

Bruno Hellendorff, a research fellow of the Asia program of the Group for Research and Information on Peace and Security, said in 2015 that China's commitment to safeguarding world peace and its path of peaceful development are welcome, and that the international community considers such commitment good news for global stability. "In order to effectively pursue missions related to anti-piracy, peacekeeping, medical support, etc., the PLA needs to invest in critical capabilities," said the scholar.

II. 90,000 Tons of Diplomacy: the Real Threat

"A lie can travel halfway around the world while the truth is putting on its shoes," Mark Twain wrote. Ironically, what he used as a metaphor has often been a reality nowadays.

A country that has a long tradition of safeguarding peace and has been practicing peace is depicted as a threat. What is more ironic, the country that spares no effort to make such a claim has the world's most powerful military forces. Its military expenditure is more than those of several other top military spenders combined. It is also the country that has most often resorted to military options — often in the name of eliminating what it said were threats. It has launched wars in this way in West Asia, North Africa and areas far away from its territory, only to destroy peace and sow the seeds of chaos.

The claim of "China military threat" has its root cause in the United States rather than China itself. To understand how and why Washington rolled out such rhetoric, it is essential to delve deep into American military thinking and defense culture. U.S. defense giant Northrop Grumman has a well-known poster featuring an image of a Nimitz-class aircraft carrier sailing through the ocean. Below the ship is text that reads “90,000 Tons of Diplomacy”. The poster is said to be visible in the Pentagon, too. It has even appeared in American pop culture in the form of a painting on t-shirts popular among youths.

Just as the Chinese people are proud of their Great Wall, the Americans take pride in their aircraft carriers. They have affectionately named these carriers, the biggest and most lethal weapons in the world, after their presidents, such as George Washington, Abraham Lincoln, John F. Kennedy and Ronald Reagan. Such a tradition of carrier worship is in line with U.S. belief in military might.

The Pentagon on its official website describes the U.S. military by highlighting the fact that it is America’s largest employer, employing 2.15 million service members and 732,079 civilians, and has approximately 4,800 defense sites in more than 160 countries on all seven continents. No other country on this planet can rival the United States in terms of projecting its military power around the world. Neither has any other country waged as many wars as the United States. Since World War II, the United States has initiated the wars on the Korean Peninsula, in Vietnam, in the Gulf region, in Kosovo, in Afghanistan and in Iraq. It has been deeply involved in conflicts in Libya and Syria. Statistics show that more than 30,000 civilians have been killed in Afghanistan since 2001. More than 180,000 civilians have been killed in Iraq since Washington invaded the country in 2003. In Syria, more than 10,000 civilians were killed in 2017 alone.

An article published on the The Diplomat site in April 2018 said that “American policymakers and military leaders, despite continuously waging war, paradoxically have a more ‘benign’ and ‘cleaner’ understanding of war.”

"This particular American Way of War, ostensibly built upon a more scientific and enlightened understanding of war and warfare, pointedly fails to take into account the full nature of conflict. Among other things, it neglects the blind forces of war, defined by Clausewitz as primordial violence, hatred, and enmity, which can only be experienced and, consequently, understood, when they hit home," the article said.

Driving the bellicose policies is political manipulation by interest groups. After World War II, the powerful U.S. military industry groups became vested interests which tended to profit from making wars and selling their weaponry. It is estimated that more than 30 percent of U.S. firms have a complicated relationship in one form or another with the military industry. Their agents can often be seen in U.S. government and Congress. Politicians are often lobbyists on their behalf and get funding support in their campaigns.

Wars make good business for the United States. A report on global arms trade published by the Stockholm International Peace Research Institute in 2018 showed that from 2013–17 the United States accounted for 34 percent of the global total in arms trade, selling to at least 98 regions and countries, much more than any other major arms exporters. As a result, the United States further consolidated its status as the world's largest arms exporter.

The country that profits from making wars and selling arms surely does not want peace. Only by fabricating and highlighting threats can it maintain its colossal defense budget that is the biggest in the world, and sell arms and military protection. This is exactly the real value of playing up the claim of China military threat. David Isenberg, a researcher at the Oslo-based Peace Research Institute, wrote in his 2009 article "US Cries Chinese Wolf" about why the United States likes to create hype over the Chinese military threat.

"Ever since the demise of the Soviet Union many members of America's politico-military-industrial sector have been looking for another country as a replacement, if only to justify the huge military and security expenditures the United States appropriates annually. And, by default, given its sheer size, population, and increasing economic importance, China is seen as the new threat standard. Indeed, China now provides the rationale for at least a quarter of the Pentagon's budget," Isenberg wrote.

The U.S. military made no secret of using the China threat hype to seek funds from Congress. During a House budget committee hearing in March 2018, senior U.S. military officials tried their best to hype China's global influence, according to a report by *The Hill*, a U.S. daily, U.S. Navy Secretary Richard V. Spencer told lawmakers, "When it comes to China, the bottom line there is the checkbook. Not only in the dollars and cents that they are writing to support their military expansion and their technological work, but what they're doing around the globe ... weaponizing capital." Spencer, in his attempt to secure military funding, referred to China's investment in Sri Lanka's Hambantota Port, an economic project, as a project with a military intent. In fact, China is in charge of only port operation but left port security to Sri Lankan authorities. The government of Sri Lanka also stressed that the port construction was conducive to the country's economic development.

President Trump signed the fiscal 2019 National Defense Authorization Act, with the defense budget at a record high of 716 billion U.S. dollars, several days before the Pentagon released the 2018 China Military Power Report. The act, of course, highlights the rivalry between the United States and China, and calls for stronger defense ties with Taiwan.

The United States tried to create hype over the so-called tensions in the South China Sea among the Southeast Asian countries, essentially an alternative form of claim of a China threat, and use it as a pretext to sell its security guarantee. In recent years, the United States deployed more than half its warships in the Pacific, tried to consolidate the U.S.-Japan and

U.S.-Philippines alliance, and staged war games in the South China Sea and nearby waters. All in all, the U.S. tries to use military pretext to create a gravity of security that pulls the related countries together under the protection of the United States. The United States itself, in the process, has achieved its purpose of rebalancing towards the Asia Pacific.

There is also a psychological need to identify a rival and fight it, as a result of the mentality of imperial hegemony. Ever since World War II, the United States has had a cornerstone national policy of maintaining its superior military power. In his inauguration speech in 2009, President Barack Obama made it clear that it is of utmost importance for the United States to make sure that it has the most powerful military force on the planet. The National Security Strategy report, released by the White House in late 2017, described China as a strategic competitor. Senior diplomat Charles Freeman, who worked as an interpreter for President Nixon on his historic China visit, noted that many in the United States saw the rise of China as a cure for the U.S. post-Cold War syndrome of lack of an enemy, but nevertheless cautioned that these people should know that China will not be a sort of global hegemony. The United States, rather, has constantly manifested its hegemonic mentality. The concerns of the United States over a far weaker military power such as China shows the determination of the United States to maintain its capability of deciding on global interests and winning wars against any and all foreign enemies, including China. The United States will not allow its military superiority be weakened to any extent even if other military powers do not represent any threat to the U.S. continent[1].

Freeman, in his new book, also cited what he thinks are some of the most shocking examples of the U.S. hegemonist mentality. Donald Rumsfeld, in an address at the Shangri-La Dialogue when he was secretary of defense, said people must question China's surprising increase in military expenditure with no threat from any other countries, but ignored the fact that U.S. military spending had been growing substantially. He publicly advocated a regime change in China and called for a more open replacement.

Rumsfeld's successors inherited his arrogance in full by not bothering to hide their hegemonist mentality, and produced more shocking incidents of such arrogance. Chuck Hagel publicly declared that the order dominated by the United States and its allies is the order of the Asia Pacific or even the world. The United States must lead on the world stage. If not, who else can lead? FBI Director Christopher Ray said in a July 2018 speech in Colorado that China is attempting to become the world's only superior ruling power and economic power, and take the place of the United States.

It is not difficult to understand why the United States has tried to portray China as a military threat in recent years, if one is aware of such the mentality of the United States. But these claims, however skillfully fabricated, are fundamentally not sustainable and would eventually break apart to reveal their true colors. Such examples abound.

The Cox Report, or Report of the Select Committee on U.S. National Security and Military/Commercial Concerns with the People's Republic of China, is a good example. It uses what "could happen in the worst scenario" and "perhaps," "maybe" or "possibly" to drive its reasoning towards the alleged theft of intelligence on U.S. nuclear technology by China, so as to divert the public attention away from the U.S. bombing of the Chinese embassy in Yugoslavia, which led to much pressure of public opinion on the United States. Evidence that emerged later showed these claims were fabricated, revealing the influence of the U.S. defense industry, the CIA and the Pentagon eagles behind the report. Indeed, not long after the release of the Cox Report, another report authored by five experts including Michael May, then director of the Center for International Security and Cooperation, offered a counterargument based on detailed critical analysis of the evidence and logic of the Cox Report. Their conclusion is that some of the facts were false, some of the conclusions cannot be confirmed and the alleged theft of U.S. nuclear secrets by China was an exaggeration. They also pointed out contradictions and appeal to emotions in the Cox Report.

In early 2013, there was suddenly hype over the so-called China cyber threat, with the United States, a country notorious for its cyberspace spying, now suddenly becoming a victim of cyber attacks. But all these ceased to be surprising when Keith B. Alexander, commander of the United States Cyber Command, testified to Congress. Alexander told the military committee of the Senate in March that year that the United States was setting up 13 offensive cyber troops to protect U.S. interests. The claim served as a pretext for expanding the U.S. cyber army.

The annual China Military Power Report is the best example of the fabricated claim of a China threat, but they often do not hold water.

After the release of the 2009 China Military Power Report, experts were quick to point out that the report tried its best to portray China as a threat but was not so successful. David Isenberg, a research fellow at the Peace Research Institute Oslo, observed that the authors of the report had not produced substantial evidence to back their claim of a China threat, and that what the report described and cited were no more than military modernization efforts which any major power would have done. In addition, statistics showed that the U.S. military budget still by far dwarfs Chinese military expenditure. What the report cited as the most imminent threat was China's projection of power in order to secure its channels of access to resources or exercise its sovereignty over disputed territories. However, the same report also said that the capability of the People's Liberation Army will still be rather limited ... in the coming decades.

The release of the 2011 China Military Power Report can actually be said to be challenging. Its submission to Congress was delayed by more than 170 days from the original plan. U.S. media said the delay was due to a fight between the different departments over how to revise the report during a review, and the purpose of the revision was to offer the largest possible support to the eagles on Capitol Hill in their campaign to prevent a cut in military budget. What Buck McKeon, then chairman of the House Armed Forces Committee, said in a statement after the release of the report showed an attempt to highlight the threat as a pretext for propping up the defense budget. If the allies of the United States, he said, ended up believing that the U.S. would reduce our deployment of troops in the Asia Pacific and cut our military presence in the region so as to cut the cost, then the security of the Asia Pacific would be further jeopardized, which is ... unacceptable.

The final report was hardly convincing even after the authors spent more than half a year to refine it. The 84-page report, U.S. experts noted, was "big on the subjunctive" and used a lot of phrases like "might disrupt," "perhaps would lead to" and "could enrich" when describing the threats, which shows that the threats were not that specific or real. The report was "not so impressive" when it comes to the actual problems that need to be dealt with. Michael Schiffer, an official at the East Asia bureau of the Pentagon, could hardly make his speech logical and organized at the press conference for the release of the report that was to be submitted to Congress, showing the inconsistency of the report. A reporter asked, "You said at the beginning that the Chinese military buildup was destabilizing ... Can you specifically say which part of that buildup is — you consider destabilizing, which aspects that you referred to?" Schiffer had to backtrack on what he said: "I think I said that it was potentially destabilizing ... "

The report also cited China's huge efforts in developing military technologies where the United States had long had an advantage, such as aircraft carriers and stealth fighters. But experts were quick to point out that "this says more about U.S. insecurities than it does about Chinese military advances".[2]

The 2015 China Military Power Report was challenged, too. After its release, Andrew S. Erickson, an associate professor of strategy at the U.S. Naval War College and a core founding member of the China Maritime Studies Institute at the college, pointed out several fallacies in the report in an article published in the bimonthly magazine *The National Interest*. The report names China "the top ship-producing nation in the world," but omits the critical qualifier that this is in terms of gross commercial tonnage — not sophistication, systems, technology or quality. Ranges quoted for anti-ship cruise missiles are not explained. Likewise unexplained is the Department of Defense's (DoD) methodology for calculating China's total military spending[3].

III. Coexisting: Wall and Carriers

The relationship between China and the United States is now one of the most important, sophisticated and delicate bilateral relationships in our world. Its course of development has a lot of influence on world peace and stability, and on future prospects of the world. It is not only necessary but possible for the two countries to coexist by trying to work together while respecting the differences that may exist between them.

An article in weekly magazine *The Economist*, in early 2018 said predictions that the United States and China are destined to fall into the Thucydides's trap are too much of a predeterminist nature. Such predictions were based on analyses of conflicts between incumbent powers and aggressive emerging challengers, but it is different in our time as China and the United States are closely interconnected by shared economic interests. The existence of nuclear arms has also reduced the risks of war between them. More importantly, the changes in the demographic trends and popular opinions in China show that members of the public in China are in no way interested in a conflict with the United States.

Dr. Henry Kissinger, in his work *On China*, advocates that Washington and China establish a relationship of "coevolution," in which both China and the United States pursue their domestic development, cooperate with each other where possible, and adjust their relations so as to minimize conflicts. Wang Jisi, director of the Center for International and Strategic Studies, Peking University, agrees with Kissinger. He thinks coevolution entails benign competition, and it is important and most constructive that the competition should eventually depend upon the ability of the two governments to address their domestic challenges and win approval from their peoples.

Wang is not the only scholar who has set out to explore the possible paradigms of benign competition between China and the United States. The academia, encouraged by the leadership, has been enthusiastically researching the topic of "a new paradigm of major power relations".

Who would think 40 years ago that a secret visit, for which even the State Secretary was kept in the dark, would eventually transform the global order? Yuan Peng, president of the China Institutes of Contemporary International Relations, wrote in his new book *From Westphalia to a New World Order* that it is important to have vision and creativity in the conduct of the relations between China and the United States, and it is fully possible for China and the United States to jointly chart a new path of major power relations.

Chinese scholars mostly agree that the new paradigm of major power relations is not imaginary but is realistically based on several already-existing prerequisites. The trends of the era are that we are increasingly multipolar in politics, globalized in economy, diverse in culture and information-driven in terms of society. There are multiple layers of communication such as the mechanism of high-level dialogue, the mechanism of trust building between the military powers of the two sides, and mechanisms of local and non-governmental exchanges. The relationship is also driven by shared interests in terms of the economy and jointly addressing international challenges.

The vast Pacific Ocean has often been used as a metaphor that there is enough space for the two major powers to coexist. It would be in the ultimate interests of our common world that aircraft carriers and the Great Wall both be jointly put to use in safeguarding peace.

[1] Charles W. Freeman. *Interesting Times: China, America and the Shifting Balance of Prestige.*

[2] David Isenberg, "Pentagon talks up the China threat", *The Asia Times*. August 31, 2011.

[3] Andrew S. Erickson, "What does the Pentagon think about China's rising military might?" *National Interest*. May 11, 2015.

Chapter Eight

Beyond Winners and Losers

Beggar thy neighbour ... that floods.

— *Mencius*

"We are not in a trade war with China ... We lost this war many years ago[1], " U.S. President Donald Trump tweeted early in the morning on April 4, 2018.

As Trump claimed, for quite a few U.S. administrations, their cooperation with China had been a zero-sum game, which resulted in their losses and was at China's advantage. What's more, the 300-billion-U.S.-dollar trade deficit each year was the proof. For some time, Trump's "Rip-off Theory" has gained much influence among American hawks who take a hard-line stance on China.

Loser or winner, is the relationship really that simple between the world's top two economies?

I. Tire that Lies

In 2009, the China tire case was fueled by the claim that the United States was losing. But time finally exposed the lie.

Between 2004 and 2008, the number of tires exported from China to the

United States increased by more than 200 percent. The U.S. trade unions therefore claimed in 2009 that workers were laid off by the cheap tires imported from China. It was since then that U.S. President Barack Obama's administration began to impose special protectionist tariffs on tire imports from China.

"The gain of Chinese workers is equal to the loss of American workers. The gain and loss of their workers corresponds to the winner and loser of the two countries." This seemingly reasonable equation proved false in just a few years.

According to a study[2] by the Peterson Institute for International Economics (PIIE), a U.S.-based economic think tank, the special protectionist tariffs on tires did secure around 1,200 jobs for U.S. tire manufacturers, but at a price — consumers were forced to buy pricier U.S.-made tires because their cheaper made-in-China ones had tariffs slapped on them. In 2011, U.S. consumers spent an extra 1.1 billion dollars on this, meaning that the cost of securing a job in the U.S. tire industry was as high as 900,000 dollars.

But the price paid by U.S. consumers went far beyond this.

As cheap Chinese tires were squeezed out of the U.S. market, the downstream U.S. retail industry which survived on the sale of cheap tires after the U.S. financial crisis was dealt a heavy blow. Consumers' spending on tires also squeezed out other expenditures. This "squeezing effect" hurt the retail industry. The PIIE study showed that the 2009 tire protectionist case has caused a loss of 3,731 jobs in the U.S. retail sector.

Seen from the perspective of job changes, the special tariffs on tires saved 1,200 manufacturing jobs, but killed 3,731 retail jobs, resulting in a net loss of 2,531 jobs in the United States. Securing one job meant losing more than two. Protecting inefficient economic sectors and practitioners who were unable to adapt to the free trade would harm more innocent domestic workers.

Policymakers in Washington can do the math.

In international economic exchanges, beneficiaries and losers are not simply subject to national administrative boundaries, but to the opposing interests of producers and consumers as well as those of the manufacturing industry and the retail industry. Special tariffs on tires protected the interests of the U.S. tire manufacturers, but hurt the interests of U.S. consumers and retailers. Conversely, while imported tires from China may harm the interests of U.S. manufacturers, they benefit U.S. consumers and the retail industry.

Simply looking at individual groups, industries and regions, people will find various examples of "America losing". In a similar sense, people can find multiple examples of "Chinese losing." Because global trade will inevitably redistribute interests among different industries, sectors and regions within a country, there will naturally be beneficiaries and "losers".

But this gain or loss is not limited by administrative boundaries. If it is necessary to judge according to national borders, economic globalization and free trade have actually brought about more "net gains" for China and the United States, meaning that the interests of each from free trade are greater than losses. The growth of free trade in tires has not only increased the "net welfare" of the Chinese, but also increased that of the Americans.

Of course, any benefit comes at a price. While the "absolute interests" of China-U.S. economic and trade cooperation are increasing, there must be a loss of "relative interests". Individuals, some industries or regions may fall victim. Such sacrifices exist in both countries. For example, steel workers in the central U.S. eastern state of Ohio had seen their jobs lost to their rivals in northern China's Hebei province — but at a price — since residents in nearby Beijing had been sacrificing their blue skies and clean air for some time. Recognizing this benefit is a prerequisite for understanding "absolute interests". It is a matter of both countries to reduce their loss of interests amid free trade and to sustain healthy trade relations.

The solution to the problem is not to completely break existing trade activities and rules, but to re-balance the interests within the framework of the rules. Both China and the United States should make greater use of their domestic policies to redistribute the benefits among affected groups, industries and regions. To attend to the interests of all parties, we need to redivide the pie, rather than completely disrupt the overall cooperation pattern for making bigger pies.

II. Looking Beyond the Business Cycle

Since 2017, many U.S. policy makers on China have focused on the word "reciprocal." Based on merely a few indicators in China-U.S. economic and trade relations at the moment, they have come to the conclusion that the United States is losing out to China.

Elon Musk, founder of the American electric car manufacturer Tesla, looked at the issue exactly from the perspective of reciprocal tariffs. He tweeted: "For example, an American car going to China pays 25% import duty, but a Chinese car coming to the US only pays 2.5%, a tenfold difference."

It is true that there was a tenfold difference in auto tariffs between the two countries when he made the point. High import tariffs pushed up the price, making it impossible for Tesla to compete directly with Chinese electric cars. Therefore, those who take a short-term view may argue that China is ripping off the United States. In a tweet on April 9, 2018, Trump wrote: "When a car is sent to the United States from China, there Is a Tariff to be paid of 2 1/2%. When a car is sent to China from the United States, there is a Tariff to be paid of 25%. Does that sound like free or fair trade. No, it sounds like STUPID TRADE — going on for years![3]"

However, if we take a long-term perspective, neither Musk's nor Trump's arguments hold up.

The numbers speak for themselves.

According to statistics from the U.S. Department of Commerce, in 2017, China exported only 58,000 vehicles to the United States, worth 1.5 billion dollars, mostly cars produced in China by foreign companies such as Ford and Volvo, with hardly any Chinese local brands.

In 2017, the United States exported 267,000 cars to China, worth 9.9 billion dollars. China is the second-largest export market for U.S. cars, only after Canada, not yet calculating the cars that American auto companies produced and sold in China. For example, in 2017, General Motors sold 4.04 million vehicles in China; Ford, 1.2 million and Musk's Tesla, more than 20,000.

If we look at a longer period of time, since the establishment of diplomatic relations between China and the United States in 1979, the export of Chinese domestic car brands to the U.S. market has remained near zero, with virtually no growth in forty years. In contrast, the past four decades have seen American auto sales in China grow dramatically to millions this year, and tens of millions in total. Forty years ago, the Chinese market meant nothing to the U.S. auto giants. However, in 2017, 45 percent of GM's global production was sold in China. For American companies, China has grown from a minuscule market to a core one in just 40 years.

History has already told us who wins and who loses. Time to look into the future.

In July 2018, Tesla got approval for setting up a wholly-owned company in Shanghai, which was expected to produce an annual 500,000 electric vehicles in two to three years. For now, Tesla imports all the cars it sells in China. But, even so, the Chinese market accounts for 20 percent of its global sales. It is not difficult to imagine how much it will rely on the Chinese market after its factory in China is put into operation.

In a longer time frame, tariff fluctuations are huge. Before 1985, China's import tariffs for complete vehicles were as high as 120-150 percent. But, starting on July 1, 2018, China's auto import tariffs were slashed to 15 percent. As the world's largest auto market and electric vehicle market, China has greater growth potential than the United States, whose market is already saturated. Constantly lowering tariffs also means that the Chinese market will definitely consume more imported cars in the future.

Unfortunately, China's domestic auto brands remain highly dependent on the local market. In particular, small passenger cars have never made their way into the U.S. market, which has remained so for 40 years. Therefore, if we only look at the auto tariff difference between China and the United States in the beginning of 2018, then the conclusion is of course that China wins over the United States. However, if we take into account the facts in the past 40 years and the future trends of Chinese and American auto companies and markets, it is self-evident that the U.S. companies benefit more than their Chinese counterparts.

The auto industry is just an example. Well-known American companies such as IBM, Qualcomm, Apple, Microsoft, and Boeing as well as relevant industries have all enjoyed tremendous benefits in China for the past 40 years. The truly competitive foreign enterprises in China would never give up the Chinese market as they value a long-term perspective over short-term gains or losses.

According to *China Business Report* 2018, the latest annual report[4] by the American Chamber of Commerce in Shanghai, the profitability of U.S. companies in China generally declined from 2011 to 2015. This partly explains why complaints from foreign companies have increased in recent years. But statistics also show that after 2015, the profitability of U.S. companies in China has rebounded. It's just natural that the economy has its ups and downs. A simplistic analysis of China-U.S. relations at a particular moment makes no sense. We need to see if sound China-U.S. economic and trade ties will benefit the vast majority of enterprises in the long run.

We will miss the bigger picture of China-U.S. trade relations if we focus only on certain indicators within a particular time without a closer look at the past and the future.

III. Not A Game Only Between Two Players

The total economic volume of China plus the United States accounts for 40 percent of that of the whole world. Also, the two countries contribute more than 50 percent to the global economic growth. While China is the world's largest production hub, the United States is an important global sales market. The two countries string together the global industrial chain and trade flows. The trade losses or benefits between China and the United States are no longer "a game between two players".

Taking the tire case mentioned above as an example, after 2009, the U.S. government imposed anti-dumping and countervailing duties on made-in-China tires. This time, researchers found that the new round of double anti-tariffs caused collateral damage among major rubber exporters in Southeast Asia, because most of the raw materials for the Chinese tires exported to the United States were imported from Southeast Asian countries. Among them, the annual loss of Indonesian rubber producers is 48 million dollars. For Thailand, the number is 42 million dollars, for Malaysia, it is 18 million dollars and for Vietnam, 4 million dollars.

A more familiar example is the American-designed and made-in-China Apple iPhone X. According to the U.S. consulting company Bernstein, the supply chain of iPhone X involves countries from all over the world. Among them, there are 52 parts suppliers in Taiwan, 44 in the United States, 41 in Japan, 19 in Chinese mainland, 16 in the European Union and Switzerland, 12 in South Korea, nine in Hong Kong, and one in Saudi Arabia.

In fact, an iPhone perfectly reflects the real picture of today's global industrial chain. Though it is designed and manufactured only in the United States and China, the suppliers involved in the production process are from everywhere in the world. An iPhone mirrors not only the China-U.S. trade relations, but also a multilateral trade network that includes many countries and is extremely complex. If a tariff war breaks out between the two countries, the effect will ripple through the network to the whole world. As a result, it is not only the U.S. Apple Company and China's Foxconn assembly plants, but also suppliers and traders across the globe that will suffer losses.

Due to the fact that trade between China and the United States involves a large number of "intermediary goods" imported from other countries, the collateral damage has been revealed. After the United States imposed tariffs on Chinese goods, South Korea's Ministry of Trade, Industry and Energy issued a warning in July 2018, saying "Korean companies are worried their exports of intermediary goods used in those items could decrease if the tariffs are imposed."[5]

The key of great powers getting along well with each other lies in an open mind.

More than 2,000 years ago, the Chinese philosopher Mencius made an incisive exposition on similar issues. Bai Gui, prime minister of Wei in China's ancient Warring States period, built a dam on the Wei's border to control floods. Bai smugly told Mencius that his achievements in water control exceeded those of the ancient sage Yu. Mencius replied: "You are wrong, sir. Yu's regulation of the waters was in accordance with the laws of water. He therefore made the four seas their receptacle, while you make the neighboring states their receptacle. Water flowing out of its channels is called an inundation. Inundating waters are a vast waste of water, and what a benevolent man detests. You are wrong, my good sir."

The United States and China are the world's largest developed and developing economies and contribute the most to global economic growth. Therefore, when the two sides discuss economic and trade problems, they should focus on the whole world instead of simply on the two countries alone; they should follow the market force of economic globalization rather than using a series of artificial means such as tariffs to hinder the spontaneous flow of international trade. Winning or losing should be seen on a global scale, not only on a scale involving two countries.

IV. Internal Issues Matter More

There is nothing wrong with Trump's high-profile slogans such as "America First" and "Make America Great Again." Be it the U.S. wish to be "great again" or China's dream of "great rejuvenation," they represent patriots' visions for prosperity and a healthy global competition born out of a sense of crisis, which are key drivers of global development.

The problem, however, lies in the delicate balance between countries' visions together with their crisis awareness. Both the United States and China are faced with complicated domestic difficulties and challenges. Pointing fingers at each other will benefit neither the United States nor China.

"U.S. President Donald Trump suffers from an acute strain of trade deficit disorder. He blames America's ills on trade deficits and the bad deals that underpin them," Stephen Roach wrote[6]. America's trade deficit with 101 countries around the world is exactly like 101 thorns in President Trump's side.

For Roach, a senior researcher at Yale University, if there is a "loss" mentality, America's enemy is more than just China, but all 101 of the world's countries. In fact, however, the problem with the United States lies with itself — a structural problem with an economy featuring high consumption but low savings, which is the root cause for trade deficits.

Nevertheless, the above-mentioned is just the tip of the iceberg when it comes to problems with the U.S. economy — an increasingly widening wealth gap, deepening regional divisions, the replacement from automation, piling government debts, inefficient health care and elder care ... but painful reflections are far less popular than finger-pointing; an enemy outside is far more inciting to the public than an enemy within.

In his book *Who are We? The Challenges to America's National Identity*, Samuel Huntington, a renowned political scientist at Harvard University, wrote, "The ideal enemy for America would be ideologically hostile, racially and culturally different, and militarily strong enough to pose a credible threat to American security." Unfortunately, although most of the problems in the U.S. economy are self-inflicted, China, with all the characteristics of the "ideal enemy" as described by the hawks, becomes the perfect scapegoat.

Having been "scapegoated," China's each and every move is monitored; any policy is misinterpreted as neatly-conceived, long-planned, and targeting the United States; and whatever the country does serves the ultimate goal of surpassing and replacing the United States. However, such a conspiracy theory "is a question of faith rather than an issue of evidence," as pointed out by Michael Barkun, a professor of political science at the U.S.-based Syracuse University.

Such an argument by trade hawks that China sought to defeat the United States through a secret, well-conceived and strictly-enforced long-term economic plan is in line with Professor Barkun's three principles for judging conspiracy theories: Nothing happens by accident. Nothing is as it seems. And everything is connected.

But is there really such a Chinese economic conspiracy

"Home is where the heart is[7]," said professor Wang Jisi. He believes China's strategic thinking involves looking more inward than outward and that the great rejuvenation of the Chinese nation is to transcend China's own tragedy in modern times, rather than to surpass the United States of today. What's more, the professor believes that China's top concern at present is to avoid the "middle-income trap."

China is not yet a rich country by the latest World Bank standards[8] in 2018. A middle-income country is one with a per capita national income between 1,006 and 12,235 U.S. dollars, among which those between 1,006 and 3,995 dollars are called middle-lower income countries. Those with per capita national income of 3,996 to 12,235 dollars are middle-higher income countries and those with more than 12,235 dollars, high-income countries.

According to World Bank data, China's per capita national income in 2016 was 6,309 dollars, compared to the 5,660 yuan (8,836 dollars according to the exchange rate of the time). China is a middle-income country by whatever standard, likely to rank among high-income countries in the future.

But breaking through the "middle-income trap" is not easy. Only 13 of the 101 middle-income economies of the 1960s became high-income economies by 2008. In other words, only one in every eight middle-income countries can rank among the high-income countries. Moreover, its status as a high-income country is not forever assured even after crossing the 12,000-dollar per capita national income threshold.

According to the U.S.-based Brookings Institution researchers Indermit Gill and Homi Kharas[9], who also coined the concept "middle-income trap," to break through such a trap, an economy needs to undergo multiple necessary transformations. The first is to smoothly pass through the Lewis turning point, transforming itself from a labor-intensive industry before the demographic dividend disappears. Second, it needs to achieve technological upgrading, guided by industrial policies. Next, a reform of the political system and the establishment of efficient and responsive government bureaucracies are necessary.

Therefore, to transcend the trap and finally realize the dream of enriching 1.3 billion people calls for continuous reform and development. This is precisely "where the heart is" in China's strategic thinking.

During the Spring and Autumn Period (770 B.C.-476 B.C.) and the Warring States Period (475 B.C.–221 B.C.) in ancient China, when the state of Lu was looking for an excuse to attack its vassal state Zhuanyu, Confucius warned, "I am afraid that for the Ji (ruler of Lu) Clan, the real threat does not come from Zhuanyu, but lies within the their own chambers" — a wisdom which has shaped how Chinese have viewed the world for thousands of years, i.e. "internal worries" are the root of all problems.

V. Widening Wealth Gap

U.S. trade hawks misinterpreted China's motives, exaggerated China's strength, and artificially created the wrong impression that China-U.S. economic and trade relations feature more competition than cooperation. For China, it is all too early to discuss the "Thucydides trap" proposed by Harvard professor Graham Allison.

As the gross domestic product (GDP) gap shrinks, the gap of per capital national wealth is still expanding. That the Chinese economy is about to surpass that of the United States is merely an illusion triggered by GDP as the sole indicator. According to the statistics of the World Bank (unit: current dollar), when China gained accession to the WTO in 2001, its per capita national income was 915 dollars compared to America's 31,985 dollars, a difference of 31,070 dollars. As of 2016, China registered 6,309 dollars compared to 49,574, a gap of 43,265 dollars.

From 2001 to 2016, the annual per capita income gap between Chinese and Americans increased by 12,195 dollars, which means that despite the narrowing gap between their economic aggregates, the wealth gap between the two countries is in fact widening.

Why? The most important thing is that China's population is nearly four times that of the United States, which means China's GDP and national income must also hit that four-time standard, which is absolutely impossible in the foreseeable future.

A reasonable assessment of the economic strength of both countries depends not only on the "quantity indicators" of GDP and national income, but also on the "quality indicators," including corporate profitability, brand value and labor productivity. In addition, the environmental and economic price of economic growth should also be taken into account. After all indices are calculated, the gap between China and the United States is far greater than that between GDP and per capita income.

There is still a long way to go before the Chinese economy comprehensively catches up with that of the United States. Obviously, when China's per capita GDP is only one-seventh of that of the United States, it's groundless to invite unnecessary worries by discussing the so-called "Thucydides trap."

Losing and winning is not a matter of simple confrontation. China-U.S. economic cooperation has never been a zero-sum game. The rise of China does not entail the decline of the United States.

The economic competition between the United States and China will certainly increase amid fast-paced globalization, but cooperation has also been deepened. Economic globalization, the multilateral trade regime, global poverty reduction, climate change ... all these global challenges are not surmountable without cooperation between the two countries. The strengthening of the "competitive cooperation" between China and the United States indicates increasingly mature China-U.S. economic and trade relations.

[1] Donald Trump Twitter: "We are not in a trade war with China, that war was lost many years ago by the foolish, or incompetent, people who represented the U.S."
[2] PIIE, *US Tire Tariffs: Saving Few Jobs at High Cost*, April 2012.
[3] Donald Trump Twitter: "When a car is sent to the United States from China, there is a Tariff to be paid of 2 1/2%. When a car is sent to China from the United States, there is a Tariff to be paid of 25%. Does that sound like free or fair trade. No, it sounds like STUPID TRADE – going on for years!"
[4] *China Business Report 2018*, The American Chamber of Commerce in Shanghai.
[5] "Collateral Damage Predicted from US-China Trade War", *Financial Times*, July 12, 2018. " 'As Chinese electronics, computers and communications equipment were included in the additional list of tariffs, Korean companies are worried their exports of intermediary goods used in those items could decrease if the tariffs are imposed,' the South Korean trade ministry said."
[6] Stephen Roach, *Donald Trump is Suffering from Trade Deficit Disorder*, March 7, 2017.
[7] Wang Jisi, "China's Search for a Grand Strategy", Feb. 2011, *Foreign Affairs.*
[8] World Bank, *Personal Income per capita data.*
[9] Indermit Gill, Homi Kharas, The Middle Income Trap Turns Ten, August 2015.

Chapter Nine

False Alarms and Tinted Glasses

Do unto others as you would have them do unto you.

—Confucius, Analects

I. A Space Station Open to the World

The European Space Agency's German astronaut Matthias Maurer has been studying Chinese for more than six years. He has a Chinese name, Ma Tian, in which he takes great pride. "My Chinese teacher told me that the Chinese meaning of Ma Tian is 'a horse in the sky.' It wants to fly high."

There is of course a good reason for Ma Tian, who is in charge of cooperation programs between the European Astronaut Center and China, to study Chinese very hard. "I hope to go to the China Space Station (CSS) to work with Chinese astronauts and astronauts from other countries."

China plans to build a manned space station around the year 2022. If the international space station operating now in orbit is decommissioned as planned in 2024, China will become the only country in the world that owns a space station.

At a ceremony held on May 28, 2018 in the Austrian capital Vienna to announce international cooperation opportunities on the CSS, China welcomed all members of the United Nations to cooperate with it to jointly use its future CSS. "The CSS belongs not only to China, but also to the world," said Shi Zhongjun, China's ambassador to the United Nations (UN) and other international organizations in Vienna.

It marked the first time such projects are open to all UN members, showcasing such Chinese concepts for international outer space cooperation as openness, peace and win-win. Priyani Wijesekera, Sri Lanka's ambassador to the UN in Vienna, believes that the CSS would benefit developing countries like Sri Lanka, which lacks financial means and expertise to launch such a project.

The international space station that is currently operating in orbit is not completely open to the international community and many countries are barred from cooperating with it. In contrast, the CSS will provide equal cooperation opportunities for the international community, particularly the developing countries. Public and private institutions, including research institutes, universities and private businesses of all UN member states, particularly developing countries, can apply for them.

Ma Tian said he was greatly impressed by the fact that not only Europeans, but any country in the world that wants to send astronauts into space can contact China via the UN and thus has the possibility of entering space.

II. Suspecting the Neighbor of Stealing an Axe

Hollywood has been open-minded in terms of acknowledging China's progress in science and technology and its spirit of openness. In recent years, it has produced at least two movies that envisage China-U.S. cooperation in space.

In *Gravity* (2013), when U.S. astronauts who are stranded in space fall into despair, China's Tiangong Space Station, which was staying dormant, becomes their last hope and they are eventually carried back to Earth by China's Shenzhou spaceship. In *The Martian* (2015), rather than passively supplying tools, the Chinese actively participate in the Martian rescue operation. The dramatic China-U.S. space cooperation plays a key role in propelling the plot's development.

However, such cooperation is almost impossible in reality for the moment at least. It is not because China is unwilling to open its space facilities to the United States, but because the U.S. authorities impose a strict restriction on China-U.S. aerospace cooperation.

The International Space Station (ISS) jointly run by the United States and other countries has been banning China from applying for cooperation. In 2011, the U.S. Congress approved the inclusion of a clause in the spending bill prohibiting the National Aeronautics and Space Administration (NASA) from engaging in any joint scientific activity with China. In 2013, Chinese scientists were barred from attending any seminars hosted by NASA's Ames Research Center. Similar incidents occurred again and again in days that followed.

The book *Lü's Commentaries of History* written more than 2,000 years ago in China's Warring States Period records a story of a man suspecting his neighbor of stealing his axe. The story goes like this: A man lost an axe. He suspected his neighbor's son had stolen it and secretly observed the boy. He watched the way the boy walked, and he felt like it was like the way a thief would walk; he observed the boy's facial expressions, and he felt they resembled those of a thief; he listened to the boy's speech, and he felt it resembled that of a thief. In short, in his eyes, the boy's each and every move was like that of a thief. Shortly afterwards, the man found his axe while digging earth. Then, he observed the boy again and his actions no longer resembled those of a thief.

In the eyes of U.S. hawks, China is just like the boy who was suspected of stealing the axe. Each of its words and actions seems to suggest that it intends to take over the United States' hegemonic position. In their logic, the Belt and Road Initiative is meant to pitch other countries against the United States; the "Made in China 2025" plan is designed to grab jobs from U.S. high-tech companies; the establishment of the Asia Infrastructure Investment Bank is aimed at replacing the international financial institutions controlled by the United States; the provision of loans to developing countries is intended to lure them into debt traps and submit them to Chinese orders, and the maritime disputes with such neighbors as Japan and the Philippines are intended to weaken U.S. allies and expel the United States from East Asia. In short, whether China carries out cooperation with other counties or is involved in disputes with other countries, whether it develops its own economy or improves its technology, they are all aimed at U.S. hegemony.

Haunted by their "inner devil," the hawks failed to see that the Chinese moves were driven by its inherent development needs and are not only reasonable, but also appropriate and legitimate.

III. Who Is Behind the Diaoyu Islands Dispute?

Indeed, the relations between China and some of its neighbors became strained over some issues in recent years. All people familiar with the truth know that none of those conflicts were started by China, which has maintained a high degree of restraint with a responsible attitude and eased all of the tensions through dialogue. It is worth noting that the influence of the United States is visible behind all these conflicts.

The China-Japan dispute over the Diaoyu Islands is a case in point.

The Diaoyu Islands have been an inherent part of Chinese territory since ancient times. While navigating the ocean and engaging in fishing, the ancestors of the Chinese were the first to discover and name the islands.

The earliest historical document available so far that records such names as the Diaoyu Islands and Chiwei Island is the book *Voyage with a Tail Wind* which was finished in 1403, the first year of the reign of Emperor Yongle of the Ming Dynasty. It shows that China already discovered and named the Diaoyu Islands over 600 years ago.

According to research by Professor Liu Jiangyong from the Institute of Modern International Relations of Tsinghua University, in the 20 years between 1874 (when Japan first invaded Taiwan) and 1894 (when the Sino-Japanese War began), all kinds of maps and literature drafted by the Navy Ministry of Japan, including one that lays out all the coastal provinces of the Qing court, identified the Diaoyu Islands, Huangwei Island and Chiwei Island as northeastern islands of Taiwan. Japan's Foreign Ministry and Army Ministry also confirmed the accuracy of those maps.[1]

On April 17, 1895, the Qing government was defeated in the Sino-Japanese War and was forced to sign the unequal treaty, the Treaty of Shimonoseki, ceding to Japan the whole island of Taiwan and its surrounding islands, which include the Diaoyu Islands.

After World War II, the Diaoyu Islands, being part of Taiwan's surrounding islands, should be returned to China according to the Cairo Declaration and the Potsdam Declaration. However, the United States took over Japan's Okinawa and included the Diaoyu Islands in Okinawa according to the so-called Treaty of San Francisco. The People's Republic of China was not involved in the treaty's preparation, drafting or signing, and thus does not recognize its legitimacy. In the early 1970s, the United States privately transferred the administration of the Diaoyu Islands to Japan, sowing the seeds of the Diaoyu Islands dispute between China and Japan.

Tensions have been running high between China and Japan over the sovereignty of the Diaoyu Islands in recent years due to provocations from

Japan. On April 16, 2012, Tokyo Governor Shintaro Ishihara announced at a seminar in the United States that the Tokyo government planned to "purchase" the Diaoyu Islands. After that, Japanese netizens called on each person to donate 10,000 yen in a campaign to fund the "purchase" of the Diaoyu Islands. On July 6, a high-ranking Japanese official visited Ishihara and told him the guidelines for "nationalizing" the Diaoyu Islands.

On Aug. 15, the Japan Coast Guard "arrested" activists from Hong Kong who had landed on the Diaoyu Islands to demonstrate for their sovereignty. On Sept. 10, the Japanese government unveiled its policy to "nationalize" the Diaoyu Islands and on the next day, signed a so-called deal on "purchasing" the islands, which angered the Chinese government and people. Since then, the Sino-Japanese confrontation over the Diaoyu Islands escalated with each passing day and bilateral ties took a sharp turn for the worse.

In this process, Washington adopted an ambiguous attitude at first. Later, as it grew more suspicious toward China, it became more and more biased toward Japan. Several high-ranking U.S. officials, including the admiral of the U.S. Pacific Command and the defense secretary, stated on various occasions that the Treaty of Mutual Cooperation and Security between the United States and Japan applies also to the Diaoyu Islands. This position was even written into a U.S.-Japan joint statement. The U.S. backing undoubtedly emboldened Japan to confront China and heightened regional tensions.

This case shows that the crux of the disputes between China and some of its neighbors lies in the fact that these countries have been challenging China's bottom line and their provocations have often won silent approval and even backing from the United States. China has not toughened its position or bullied its smaller neighbors after its national strength increased. All China has done is simply to make maximum efforts to safeguard its legitimate rights while trying to exercise restraint, and has not in the least tried to challenge the hegemony of the United States.

Such examples abound. The South China Sea issue is one of them.

IV. Only Dialogue Can Solve Problems

The South China Sea Islands are China's inherent territory. Chinese people's activities in the South China Sea date back to over 2,000 years ago. China is the first to have discovered, named, explored and exploited the South China Sea Islands and relevant waters, and the first to have continuously, peacefully and effectively exercised sovereignty and jurisdiction over them.

After the end of World War II, China recovered and resumed exercising sovereignty over the South China Sea Islands, which were invaded and illegally occupied by Japan during its war of aggression against China.

China drew a map with a dotted line of the South China Sea to mark its territory and made it known to the world in 1948.

Since the 1970s, the Philippines has illegally occupied by force some islands and reefs of China's Nansha Islands, giving rise to the territorial dispute between the two countries.

The Philippines built military facilities on some islands and reefs it has seized, willfully destroyed survey markers set up by China, and attempted to illegally occupy China's Ren'ai Reef by using a military vessel running aground on it.

The Philippines has carried out illegal oil and gas exploratory drilling and bidding in the waters of the Nansha Islands, and has repeatedly harassed and attacked Chinese fishermen and fishing boats conducting routine fishing operations.

The Philippines has also raised territorial claims on China's Huangyan Island (Huangyan Dao) in the South China Sea, attempted to occupy it illegally and deliberately caused the Huangyan Dao Incident.

On April 10, 2012, a Philippine naval vessel entered the waters off

Huangyan Island and harassed Chinese fishermen who were taking shelter from a storm in the lagoon. It once attempted to capture and detain Chinese fishermen, but was thwarted by two Chinese maritime surveillance vessels which had arrived upon learning the news. The two countries' vessels then had a face-off on the sea in the Huangyan Dao area for more than two months.

In January 2013, the Philippine government unilaterally initiated the South China Sea arbitration, breaching the China-Philippines agreement to solve disputes through bilateral negotiations and thus aggravating the conflicts between the two sides and escalating the tension in the South China Sea.

Facts have proven that confrontation will not lead to a peaceful resolution of the South China Sea issue, while only friendly consultations truly benefit the people of the countries concerned.

On July 12, 2016, the Hague-based Permanent Court of Arbitration ruled in favor of the Philippine side in the South China Sea case. The situation took another twist as the new Philippine President Rodrigo Duterte, who took office in June 2016, changed his country's stance on the South China Sea issue by adopting an attitude of carrying out dialogue and cooperation with China, which immediately eased the tense situation in the South China Sea and created an opportunity for the two countries to resume cooperation in all fields.

In 2017, the trade volume between China and the Philippines topped 50 billion U.S. dollars for the first time, making China the Philippines' No. 1 trading partner and source of imports, and the fourth largest export market. In the same year, China became the Philippines' second largest source of tourists, with Chinese tourists making nearly 1 million visits to the Southeast Asian country, doubling the number in 2016.

In the past two years, China has provided the Philippines with 1.27 billion Chinese renminbi (183 million U.S. dollars) of free financial aid and concessional loans of 10 billion U.S. dollars. Moreover, the construction of two Chinese-financed drug rehabilitation centers is underway. China has also provided material support to help the Philippines tackle climate change.

At the beginning of 2017, the two countries formally established a bilateral consultation mechanism on the South China Sea issue, returning to the right track of solving related maritime issues through consultation. Both sides have set up technical working groups under the consultation mechanism with an aim to exchange views on ways of maritime cooperation, which covers recent developments that affect political security in the South China Sea, maritime search and rescue, maritime security, marine environmental protection, marine scientific research and fishing.

The two sides are also looking into joint maritime oil and gas exploration on the condition that their respective sovereignty, sovereign rights and jurisdiction are not undermined.

At the 21st China-ASEAN (10+1) leaders' meeting held in Singapore in November 2018, China and some ASEAN (Association of Southeast Asian Nations) countries committed themselves to finalizing the Code of Conduct in the South China Sea in three years, which is of great significance for the long-term peace, stability and order in the South China Sea.

It's normal for countries to have territorial disputes. What counts is how they solve such disputes. Unlike the West, which frequently resorts to force, China prefers to resolve conflicts through such peaceful means as dialogue and cooperation. "In practicing the rules of propriety, it is harmony that is prized," the Chinese philosopher Confucius said in the Analects more than 2,000 years ago. The success story of China and the Philippines turning hostility into friendship is a good case in point.

China-Japan relations experienced similar twists and turns. On Oct. 25, 2018, Japanese Prime Minister Shinzo Abe embarked on an official visit to China, the first by a Japanese prime minister in seven years, which showed that bilateral ties were back on the right track thanks to diplomatic efforts by both sides following a series of disturbances caused by disputes over the Diaoyu Islands.

V. Great Countries Perish Through Belligerence

"The Methods of the Sima"is a book on the art of war written in the Western Zhou Dynasty in ancient China, before the Spring and Autumn Period and the Warring States Period and before the world-renowned *The Art of War*. The first chapter of the book is titled "Benevolence is the root," and expounds a benevolence-centered war concept. At the beginning of the book it says that countries, however great they may be, perish through belligerence.

Solving problems through dialogue is a natural choice for China and manifests China's traditional values that have existed since ancient times. China does this with the Philippines, Japan and also other countries that have territorial disputes with China, like India and Vietnam.

Although China's comprehensive national and military strength far exceeds that of most of its neighboring countries, China has always adhered to the principle of peaceful development and good-neighborliness, and exercised maximum restraint even on issues concerning its core interests such as territorial sovereignty. Only when seriously threatened or even infringed upon by others will China take necessary actions to defend itself.

On June 18, 2017, Indian border troops crossed the China-India boundary in the Sikkim sector at the Duo Ka La (Doka La) pass into Chinese sovereign territory. The reasons later given by the Indian side included that Dong Lang (Doklam) belongs to Bhutan and that China's road construction in the Dong Lang area brings security risks to India.

The incident, in which the Indian border troops illegally crossed the Sikkim sector of the border jointly recognized by China and India, was essentially different from previous frictions and face-offs between the border troops of both sides. The excuses the Indian side used to justify its action are untenable. First, although the border between China and Bhutan has not been finalized, the two sides have been making efforts to resolve the issue through peaceful negotiations, during which no third party should intervene. Second, China's construction of roads in the Dong Lang area is a sovereign act on its own territory, which is completely legitimate and other parties should not intervene in this activity. In the past few decades, it has been the Indian side that has built a large number of facilities in the Sikkim sector of the border, with a large number of troops deployed. In some places, the Indian side even built military facilities such as pillboxes on or over the borderlines, constantly changing the status quo in the border areas.

China-India ties were negatively affected by the Indian border troops' illegal crossing of the border, which caused a long face-off with the Chinese border troops. China exercised a high degree of self-restraint and refrained from using force in the face of India's clear violation of international law and its unreasonable arguments, firmly insisting on resolving the crisis through diplomatic means.

On Aug. 28, 2017, after over two months of diplomatic efforts, the Indian defense personnel and equipment were eventually fully pulled back to the Indian side of the border, marking a peaceful resolution of this incident.

The composure and patience demonstrated by China in this incident also seemed to have led India to reflect on its China policy. In April 2018, Chinese President Xi Jinping and Indian Prime Minister Narendra Modi held an informal meeting in the central Chinese city of Wuhan in Hubei Province. Modi said the meeting was of historic significance, and that maintaining frequent high-level exchanges and strategic communication between the two sides was conducive to enhancing mutual understanding and bilateral cooperation, which is in line with the common interests of the two countries as well as regional development and prosperity. He said the Indian side was willing to work with China to this end.

Peace and stability in the Asia-Pacific region have been fundamentally safeguarded thanks to China's strategic composure and persistence in solving problems through dialogue and negotiations.

VI. Sowing Discord Endangers Stability

It is not difficult to notice that both Ishihara's offer to "purchase"the Diaoyu Islands and the Philippine military vessels' harassment of Chinese fishing boats in waters off the Huangyan Island happened in April 2012, which was shortly after the U.S. government's high-profile announcement of its "Pivot to Asia" strategy at the end of 2011.

When U.S. President Barack Obama took office in 2009, he believed that the United States had invested too many resources in and paid too much attention to Iraq and Afghanistan, while Asia was more important to the future of his country. In October 2011, then Secretary of State Hillary Clinton published an article titled "America's Pacific Century" in *Foreign Policy* magazine, claiming that "One of the most important tasks of American statecraft over the next decade will therefore be to lock in a substantially increased investment — diplomatic, economic, strategic, and otherwise — in the Asia-Pacific region."[2]

A month later, Obama formally announced the United States' "Pivot to Asia" strategy at the annual gathering of leaders of the Asia-Pacific Economic Cooperation (APEC) in Hawaii. The strategy was later restated as "Rebalance to Asia-Pacific." A major outcome of the strategy is that Washington will deploy 60 percent of its naval and air forces to the Asia-Pacific before 2020. Such a strong military deployment is apparently not aimed at dealing with countries like the Democratic People's Republic of Korea (DPRK) or Vietnam.

Seen from a Chinese perspective, the U.S. policy shift and some Asia-Pacific countries' provocations against China's territorial sovereignty are interconnected: Either Washington's hyping of the "China Threat Theory" provoked the latter's worries, or the latter was using Washington's growing vigilance against China for its own gains, or both were true.

The United States has always stressed that its presence in the Asia-Pacific safeguarded peace in the region. Yet in fact, its current behavior has done more to sow discord between China and other Asia-Pacific countries.

A most obvious example is the U.S. military's so-called "freedom of navigation" campaign in the South China Sea. Although China and other relevant parties of the South China Sea issue were seeking a peaceful solution through dialogue, and had achieved remarkable progress in some areas, the United States seemed unwilling to see the situation defuse again. It kept provoking China by sending warships and warplanes into waters and airspace off Chinese islands, trying to deter its allies from compromising with China.

Such moves to strenuously test China's bottom line were apparently not conducive to peace and stability in the South China Sea, but only aggravated the risks for stoking more regional tensions. Maybe that was exactly what the hawks in the United States wanted to see.

John Ross, senior fellow at the Chongyang Institute for Financial Studies at Renmin University of China and a former policy director of Economic and Business Policy for Ken Livingstone, mayor of London, wrote in his book *The Great Chess Game? A New Perspective on China's Destiny*: "But to some groups, especially to American neo-conservatives who have a clear goal of maintaining the U.S. status as the world's biggest economy and most powerful country, even the Chinese citizens' basic goal of achieving prosperity is completely unacceptable. Their plan means that even if China's living standard reaching a quarter of the United States' is unacceptable. Undoubtedly, the Chinese will never accept that they keep a low living standard for a long time, especially to secure another country's hegemony. So the American neoconservatives' plan will necessarily increase potential tensions in the global situation."[3]

China never has a strategic intention to pursue hegemony or replace the United States. However, there are some American politicians who attempt to reshape or contain China according to their own will.

"Our policy will seek to facilitate a peaceful evolution of China from communism to democracy by encouraging the forces of economic and political liberalization in that great country," Warren Christopher said about the Clinton administration's foreign policy in his statement before the Senate Foreign Relations Committee on Jan. 13, 1993, at a hearing to confirm his secretary of state nomination.[4]

In 2001, shortly after taking office, the Bush administration called China a rival to the United States rather than a strategic partner. During his first term as president, Obama also launched his "Pivot to Asia"plan targeting China.

Such remarks and actions, to whatever degree they were based on consideration for domestic electoral factors, sent a clear signal to China and the world: The United States does not trust China, and is dissatisfied with China's growing strength or political system. Hence, the United States wanted to send more military forces to the Asia-Pacific to be deployed on island chains and important maritime traffic channels surrounding China, so as to "protect peace in the Asia-Pacific."

Conversely, if China continuously criticized the U.S. political system, viewed the United States' growing strength as a severe threat, set up hundreds of military bases in the United States' neighboring countries to "protect American security" and deployed a large number of warships, warplanes and ground forces there, what would the U.S. side think?

VII. Inevitable Disillusionment

Nowadays, some U.S."China hands" are said to feel disillusioned about

China, as China did not change in the way envisaged by American strategists. In fact, such feelings of failure and disillusionment are merely the result of a decades-old illusion destroyed.

Time has proved that the "China Collapse Theory" has collapsed. But those holding the "China Threat Theory" then packaged China with a new "fraudulent theory" to cover up the erroneousness of their original opinion. Their hidden meaning is: It is not that we are incompetent, but our rival is too cunning.

As a matter of fact, many rational U.S. scholars can clearly see the direction China is developing in and the West's misconceptions about China by proceeding from an objective point of view and dispelling ideological bias.

The American writer Laurence Brahm, who came to study in China in the early 1980s and experienced China's reform and opening-up first-hand, wrote in his book *An Incredible Journey — Reflections on Forty Years of China's Reform and Opening-up*: "The West often looks at China with misunderstanding and prejudice. When many misunderstandings and prejudices come together, they become a cage that distorts China's domestic affairs and changes. The West's views of China often appear to be limited by this cage. The Chinese called this phenomenon 'wearing tinted glasses to see the world.' Unfortunately, the West's cage will not come down easily because it originates in the accumulation of misleading information for several hundred years, the self-proclaimed justice in their faith and the superiority of colonizers."[5]

In 1996, Brahm wrote the book *China As No. 1: The New Superpower Takes Center Stage*, predicting that China will rise as an economic power. In that year, China's gross domestic product (GDP) was merely a little over one tenth of that of the United States. In 2001, he wrote another book called *China's Century*. In the same year, the Chinese American Gordon G. Chang published *The Coming Collapse of China*. The latter became a New York Times best seller, while the former garnered little attention in the United States.

Talking about the future of China-U.S. ties, Brahm told a story: "I know the famous U.S. astronaut Edgar Mitchell well. Before he passed away, we used to hang out together quite a lot. He frequently said to me: 'If American politicians could go to space and see the world, they would know that the world is really small. In the vast universe, our planet, our world is like a small airplane. Just like flying an airplane, if two pilots have a disagreement, how could you fly it? Everyone's life is on the line as we are on the same plane. The world's population is getting bigger, yet the resources are getting fewer. The pressure is mounting. So we badly need leaders who have foresight and can consider the connectivity of all things. In terms of that, I very much agree with President Xi's concept of building a community of a shared future for mankind.'"

[1] Wang Zhuolun, Interview: Chinese scholar refutes Japan's released "historical documents" over Diaoyu Islands, Xinhua News Agency, May 13, 2016.
[2] Hillary Clinton, "America's Pacific Century", *Foreign Policy*, Nov. 2011.
[3] John Ross, *The Great Chess Game? A New Perspective on China's Destiny*, Jiangsu Phoenix Art Publishing House, April 2016, p.2.
[4] Warren Christopher, Statement before the Senate Foreign Relations Committee, Jan. 13, 1993.
[5] Laurence Brahm, *An Incredible Journey, Reflection on Forty Years of Reform and Opening-up of China*, China Commerce And Industry United Publishing House, 2018, p.6.

Chapter Ten

Chimerica and Community

Two are better than one, because they have a good reward for their toil.

— The Bible

I. Everything is Nothing

It is a big figure — the U.S.-China trade volume in 2017 was about 636 billion dollars according to the U.S. Commerce Department.[1] The figure released by China was a bit lower, at 583.6 billion dollars.[2] The difference was largely due to technical factors such as statistical caliber. But even based on the Chinese statistics, it is safe to say that the bilateral trade was huge.

That's only one of the indicators of the close economic ties between the two countries. By the end of 2017, the accumulated U.S. direct investment in China surpassed 256 billion dollars, and China's accumulated direct investment in the United States reached 140 billion dollars.[3] Every year, more than 2 million Americans travel to China, and nearly 3 million Chinese visit the United States.

Perhaps you also know that the leading U.S. fast-food chain KFC has more than 5,000 stores in China. The red-colored "Make America Great Again" baseball cap worn by Trump during the election campaign was made in China. And many Chinese teenagers regard former NBA stars such as Michael Jordan and Kobe Bryant as their idol and are almost as passionate as their U.S. peers about heroes in the Marvel Universe such as Iron Man and Hulk.

Imagine looking down over the Pacific from the sky above. The flows of goods, capital, people, information, knowledge and culture between the two sides of the ocean are like densely woven golden thread that connect the United States and China, the two largest economies in the world.

However, facing such an exciting scene, some people are frightened.

"What if China stops producing daily necessities for the U.S. one day?" "From satellites to cruise missiles, from drones to mobile phones, many components are made in China, and the U.S. lifeline is in the hands of the Chinese!" "China will soon overtake the United States, and by then we will be forced to follow their tempo."...

Therefore, the two countries must be separated and must be "decoupled!" The increasingly close and multidimensional connection and "binding" with China is not a good thing for the United States!

Many people are curious about the clouds in the sky. Looking from afar, they have a huge form but there is nothing concrete in them. Similarly, one can perhaps use "Everything is Nothing" to describe the fear and even the horror over the close relations between the two countries. Emotional speculation and hypothesis can distort our understanding of the world, and the actions it triggers often lead to unexpected results.

"Fear always springs from ignorance," says a proverb. Why would China stop production and exportation to the United States? China, which has become a manufacturing base for the whole world, is now working on overcapacity.

Yes, overcapacity. It means that China produces more than its domestic consumption needs. Against such a background, why would China give up the United States, the world's largest market? China said its export to the United States in 2017 totaled 429.7 billion dollars[4], representing an important and significant source of income for Chinese companies and individuals. From the perspective of the Chinese economy, export is still an important growth engine.

As for electronic components, those produced in China are inexpensive and of good quality, but they are by no means irreplaceable. Besides China, there are several economies with an edge in this area, such as Italy, Germany, the Republic of Korea, Japan, China's Taiwan, etc. Many of them are "old friends" of Washington. Not to mention that many manufacturers in China are actually owned by U.S. companies, or the core technologies are controlled by the U.S. side.

Will China surpass the United States soon? This trend looks possible in terms of economic aggregates.

In 2017, the U.S. GDP exceeded 19 trillion dollars, while China's approached 12 trillion dollars.[5] But if you think about it, you will know that this is just a "game of numbers." The economic aggregates of Luxembourg and Guatemala are similar, but the levels of development and affluence of the two countries are obviously different. China is still struggling to cross the "Middle Income Trap" as estimates show that China's per capita GDP just exceeded 10,000 dollars in 2018. Meanwhile, the per capita GDP of the United States has already surpassed 60,000 dollars.[6]

In terms of strategic reserve, the U.S. government had a gold reserve that is 4.4 times that of China as of November 2017[7]. And the only real global currency is the dollar, not the Chinese RMB. The United States has the most of the world's top 500 companies and is home to a number of the world's best universities, with China's top Tsinghua University standing at only around 50th place in global university ranking. Anyone who plays war video games such as World of Warships would know that the United States has 11 aircraft carriers, and China has one operational carrier, another undergoing sea trials and a third under construction.

The United States is in a stronger position than China in a comprehensive way, from financial resources to the number of multinational corporations; from scientific and technological strength to military strength; from the educational level to the influence of their respective culture. Therefore, it is not likely that the United States will have to dance to the tune dictated by China.

II. Teammate is Needed

As the U.S.-China ties grow increasingly closer and stronger, the United States remains in an advantageous and autonomous position, and has never suffered any heavy loss. President Trump said that China has taken great advantage of the United States in trade, and he even gave a concrete figure — 375 billion dollars annually.[8] But he did not tell people that trade deficit, without considering the huge controversy surrounding the figure, does not equal profit loss. Neither did he give any evidence of the U.S.-claimed net loss.

In fact, many people, including Trump, either deliberately choose to avoid mentioning or fail to realize the fact that the United States and China — the world's top two economies — have formed a deeply integrated "super symbiont" that exerts major systematic influence on the whole world, bringing benefits to both sides in a typical win-win case. This symbiont is more like a growing baby conceived by the force of Yin and Yang, instead of one being a host and the other being a parasite. Any rough measure to cut such a symbiont and the numerous "blood vessels" between the United States and China will most likely cause economic stagnancy on both sides and the re-emergence of a global recession.

As early as March 2007, Harvard Business School professor Niall Ferguson mentioned the phenomenon of the coexistence of the United States and China in his article published in the British newspaper "Sunday Telegraph" under the title of "Not two countries, but one: Chimerica."

In Ferguson's description, Chimerica is "quite a place: just 13 percent of the world's land surface, but a quarter of its population and fully a third of its economic output. What's more, Chimerica has accounted for around 60 percent of global growth in the past five years … East Chimericans are savers; West Chimericans are spenders. East Chimericans do manufactures; West Chimericans do services. East Chimericans export; West Chimericans import. East Chimericans pile up reserves; West Chimericans obligingly run deficits, producing the dollar-denominated bonds that the East Chimericans crave. As in all good marriages, the differences between the two halves of Chimerica are complementary."

The financial crisis erupted in the United States in 2008. Some assumed that Chimerica would be severely damaged. Yet the reality was that new changes occurred to Chimerica, and brought new benefits to both sides and made their links even stronger.

In the late spring of 2008, Henry Paulson, then the U.S. president's special envoy and treasury secretary, met with then Chinese Premier Wen Jiabao. The Chinese leader expressed worries about the huge debt risks of two U.S. government-sponsored agencies — Fannie Mae and Freddie Mac. Billions of dollars of Chinese investment in the United States could suffer heavy loss. So would China's economic departments exporting goods and services to the United States.

Based on the considerations of both China's domestic situations and the reluctance to see even greater problems in the U.S. economy triggering a chain reaction across the globe, Beijing unveiled a fiscal stimulus plan worth 4,000 billion yuan (579 billion dollars) to maintain overall demand levels, and did not dump the U.S. bonds it had. This indeed saved the United States by helping its multinationals survive domestic defeat, and allowed the world to remain confident in macroeconomics.

In the process of resisting financial and economic crisis, Chimerica, which had been developing on the basis of interdependence and mutual benefit, demonstrated greater strength, and greater significance to both the United States and China, as well as to the whole world.

Reflecting on that not-so-distant history, U.S. economics observer Zachary Karabell said in his book *Superfusion: How China and America Became One Economy and Why the World's Prosperity Depends On It* that if not for the multibillion dollar investment by China in the United States, the U.S. government's ability to handle the crisis would have been more restrained. Liquidity injected by central banks of different countries is highly dependent on those surplus countries, among which China contributed the most. It is this funding that prevented the complete collapse of the financial system of the United States as well as that of the whole world.

Looking forward, an above-mentioned U.S. scholar, who knows both the United States and China very well — Stephen Roach, senior fellow at Yale University's Jackson Institute for Global Affairs – further enriched the contents of Chimerica: China is the world's top exporter, which needs U.S. consumers and enterprises to meet its external demands. At the same time, the United States relies on the low-cost imports from China to help its citizens with limited incomes make a living. China is the third-largest export market of the United States and its fastest-growing export market, as well as the country which owns the most U.S. bonds and other U.S.-dollar assets. Such a reality decides that China's support is vital for the United States to deal with its long-term fiscal deficit.

Yes, a large number of people cheer for Trump's tax reduction policy, and feel excited for his magnificent project to revitalize the U.S. infrastructure. Yet, with less revenue, how could Washington be able to fund such high-cost projects? Where does the money come from.

The budget is always restrained, but the ambitious politicians and federal and municipal administrators will press forward. When California Governor Jerry Brown announced his ambitious "Green California" project, and set the timetable for "zero emission" transportation, maybe he was also thinking about finding manufacturers and suppliers which are able to meet demands on time limit, green protocols and budget.

When Brown visited China in 2013, he traveled from Guangzhou to Shenzhen in an electric car made by China's leading new energy automobile manufacturer BYD. Brown excitedly told media that California planned to have 1 million new energy automobiles on the roads by 2015, saying that he had no idea how to achieve this goal until he decided to cooperate with BYD.

When the first BYD-manufactured electric bus rolled off the line in Lancaster, California, Brown was on-site. The bus, which can carry 31 passengers, takes only three hours to be fully charged. It has a range of 250 km, produces no emission and is assembled in California (a perfect combination of creating jobs and controlling cost).

Brown put forward the "Green California" plan with an aim to make a difference regarding climate and environmental issues that he cares about. Undoubtedly, California has Tesla, and it could also find electric cars in Japan. However, to balance quality, productivity and budget, the "China plan" may be the best choice. No matter how strong LeBron James is in the NBA, he still needs some powerful teammates who earn less salaries than he does. Otherwise the championship ring will always be too far to reach. By embracing Chimerica — a combination of two major powers — Brown will probably taste the "sweet fruit" in the end.

In the current world, where the economic system in each country and the global industry chain have become increasingly complex, and geographic barriers keep being broken, it is not necessary for a country to produce all the products. Neither does a country have enough resources or ability to address all the challenges, even major countries like the United States and China. Former U.S. President Barack Obama said that the United States could not solve all its problems with its door closed.

Nowadays, it seems that the current U.S. government is moving to shut its door and sever itself from the rest of the world, especially China. You will hear claims by U.S. politicians that terrifying China has hollowed out the U.S. industries and deprived the U.S. workers of their jobs, and that increasing tariffs on billions of dollars of Chinese imports could balance the trade. However, these politicians choose to keep silent over the fact that due to these fresh tariffs the prices of many products are on the rise in the United States, and the supply chains of some industries and companies have been disrupted. Or they have to face higher cost, at least, due to the rising prices of raw materials.

Statistics of the U.S. Department of Labor showed that the prices of washing machines and dryers grew by 20 percent in the United States in the second quarter of 2018, the largest quarterly increase for the past 12 years.

According to London-based global information provider IHS Markit, in July 2018, U.S. enterprises raised their product prices at the fastest speed over the past nine years. The companies include Coca-Cola, 3M and Kraft Heinz, etc.

American home appliances manufacturer Whirlpool Corporation has long been complaining that the cost of steel in the United States has increased to "an incredible level." The company had to raise the prices of its products only to find its sales affected. Whirlpool lost over 600 million dollars in the second quarter of 2018, and its profits in 2018 were much lower than expected.

Fake fear of China in the United States leads to alienation of and resistance to the Asian nation, which in the end produces lose-lose results that harm both countries. It is just that the first part of the chain is wrong.

If one has the in-depth historical vision and broad global vision that are revealed by Karabell in "Superfusion," this unreasonable fear may be dispelled soon:

"Even if by some unexpected twist China manages to evolve over the next three decades without losing more of its autonomy and sovereignty in a world of open markets, that doesn't mean that it will then become an enemy or that the relationship with the United States will become antagonistic. And slipping behind China will not necessarily spell the end of the United States as a viable, energetic society. In truth, as lost as Britain was for several decades after 1945, it managed to remain a prosperous country with considerable standing in the world, even if it was no longer the most powerful nation. There are worse fates than to be Britain after 1945."[9]

Karabell also thinks that China and the United States are two fundamental members of Chimerica, but not all. Many European corporations also play important roles. Besides, resource-abundant nations ranging from those in Latin America to Australia to Russia, as well as companies in these countries, also play significant roles. Chimerica has become a global phenomenon, which has global influence.

Karabell has raised a fundamental point — a healthy competition between the United States and China is a blessing to the world; if the two nations fall into the so-called Thucydides's trap, a new Cold War would happen. Nobody would want to see another all-consuming Iron Curtain.

III. Humanity for a Shared Future

"More powerful than the mighty armies is an idea whose time has come," said renowned French writer Victor Hugo.

Primarily, the future of Chimerica is determined by how the two countries wish to build their relations. It is a matter of "believe it or not." The attitude toward integration and the way in which the United States and China do so will decide whether the world can enjoy long-lasting peace and prosperity in the future.

Unfortunately, the United States is showing a stronger inclination toward "detachment" and "not believe it." It has gone further to disapprove China's global vision, as many Americans tend to believe that China will make massive changes to the world to fit its own requirements once it achieves global dominance. Well, it is nothing more than a misunderstanding and misjudgment.

If you travel to China around Spring Festival or the Chinese New Year, you may find New Year paintings with two children on them — one holding a lotus flower, the other holding a box. They are known as He-He Er Xian, translated as the Two Immortals of Harmony and Union. (He and He are homophonous of lotus flower [hé] and box [hé] in Chinese.) The idea of harmony and unity has left a deep mark in traditional Chinese culture, and is also one of the cultural factors based on which that the Chinese leadership initiated the notion of "a community with a shared future for mankind."

China does not have the gene to become an aggressive or hegemonic country. It will not seek to assimilate others even if it one day tops the world in overall strength or influence. The reason is that China, an exponent of harmony in diversity, understands that "Things are born to be different" (advocated by great philosopher of ancient China, Mencius), believes in "universal love and non-offense" (advocated by great philosopher of ancient China, Mo Zi), and wishes that "peace and harmony should prevail" (written in the *Book of Documents*).

Similar thoughts exist in the West.

"There are no two leaves perfectly alike," Gottfried Wilhelm Leibniz, one of the greatest thinkers and mathematicians in the Western world, told his admirer Her Electoral Highness the Princess Sophie, when explaining the difference and the commonness of things.

"I infer ... that there are not in nature two real, absolute beings indiscernible from each other," Leibniz stated in Ibid, his fifth paper, in reinforcing the argument.

But Leibniz also admitted that they are all leaves anyway.

The planet we live on is a place of 6 billion dwellers, some 220 countries, 2,500-plus nations and over 4,000 languages. Yet, with different historical backgrounds, cultural traditions, social mechanisms, ideologies, values and temperaments, we are all human beings of the Earth.

There might be the possibility of moving to the moon or Mars in the future, but for most of us, we will stay on this blue planet. We may easily be put into unknown danger if we fail to address the ecological risks caused by the conflict between human beings and nature, the intelligent risks caused by the conflict between human beings and machines, the humanitarian risks caused by the conflict between human beings and society, the moral risks caused by the conflict between human beings themselves, the spiritual risks caused by the conflict between someone and his mind, and the value risks caused by conflict between civilizations.

In September 2015, the world was horrified to see the photo of a toddler found lying face-down on a Turkish beach. The photo is probably one of the most heart-wrenching pictures in modern history.

Though it is hard to determine who is to blame for such a tragedy, people realize that the issue of immigration can never be solved once and for all by only a group of people or by merely a certain number of countries.

In July 2018, through the lens of National Geographic, millions of people saw an extremely emaciated polar bear searching for food in an abandoned oil can. In the video posted on social media, the animal's gray fur wobbled at every step, resembling a hanging bed sheet. Even more heart-wrenching were photos of an adult polar bear chasing and cannibalizing its own cubs. Polar bears face an existential threat due to climate change, a growing lack of food and melting sea ice.

Children and baby animals ... Yuval Noah Harari said in his best-selling book, *A Brief History of Humankind*, that Homo Sapiens were merely insignificant species not worth mentioning 70,000 years ago, living in various locations in Africa. But in the next thousands of years, they became the master of the whole world and a nightmare of the global ecosystem. Even though they have increased food output, built cities, established empires and invented a trade network that reaches almost every corner of the world, they seem to have failed in reducing the pain of the world. The great leap in the overall capabilities of mankind does not necessarily translate into the improvement of each individual's livelihood.

Systematic challenges for the entire human race are just in front of us. If the smartest species on the planet (also the most arrogant on the planet) remains slow on the uptake, remains selfish and only views its peers as competitors or even enemies, the only home that we have in the universe may be put in danger.

The synergy of humankind is the only power that can lead the ark of human civilization to a brighter future. In Chinese, there is an old saying, "Where many help to gather firewood, the flames shoot high." It bears the same meaning as "United we stand, divided we fall."

The word "community" has the prefix "com," which means "with, together or in association," occurring in loanwords from Latin, and its latter part comes from "munis," of Etruscan origin, which means "to endow, to take charge of."

As a matter of fact, it is an instinct for humans, as a social animal, to form a community. And it is this ability to shoulder responsibility in a joint manner that makes them excel and reach the top of the biological chain.

As individuals, each person has the gene of being selfish, yet they also possess the gene of altruism so as to survive as a species. The balance between egocentrism and altruism is achieved through the experience obtained from the competition for survival and education.

Today, the abundance of materials allows mankind to abandon warfare, achieve better coexistence and collaboration, and jointly build the world into a place of sustainable growth and establish a healthier system for mankind.

Admit it or not, the idea of a community of a shared future for mankind is what we need in building a better tomorrow. Whether it was proposed by China or any other nation, the need is becoming all the more pressing.

The Tower of Babel in Genesis is an origin myth meant to explain why the world's peoples speak different languages. But in today's world, communication between people is without barriers.

Every day, tens of millions of Chinese read information from the West or talk to people from the United States, the United Kingdom, Canada and Australia via mobile devices. In the United States, the use of the Chinese language gets increasingly more popular, and changes in China is no longer as unclear as the dense mist over the horizon.

The major languages are increasingly intertwined and impacting one another. Moreover, the language of binary (binary code) is used globally in building a better real and virtual world for all dwellers of the Earth.

The evolvement of human civilization has entered a new era. It is time for all of us to abandon selfishness and walk hand in hand toward a shared future. We do not have a second choice.

[1] Data released by U.S. Commerce Department on Feb. 6, 2018.
[2] Data released by China's customs on Jan. 12, 2018.
[3] *Two-Way Street: 2018 Update U.S.-China Direct Investment Trends* released by U.S. Rhodium Group in April 2018.
[4] Data released by China's customs on Jan. 12, 2018.
[5] IMF World Economic Outlook, April 2018. https://www.imf.org/en/Publications/WEO/Issues/2018/03/20/world-economic-outlook-april-2018.
[6] Data on website of World Bank, March 2018. https://www.imf.org/external/datamapper/NGDPDPC@WEO/OEMDC/ADVEC/WEOWORLD/USA.
[7] https://www.gold.org/goldhub/data/monthly-central-bank-statistics.
[8] Trade Policy Agenda and 2017 Annual Report of the President of the United States on the Trade. Agreements Program, the Office of the U.S. Trade Representative, March 2018.
[9] Zachary Karabell, Wu Xue, *Superfusion: How China and America Became One Economy and Why the World's Prosperity Depends on It*, Citic Press, First Edition, May 2010.

This book is the result of a co-publication agreement between China Social Sciences Press (China) and Paths International Ltd (UK)

Title: Fake Fear: America and China Relations
Author: Xin Jiyan
ISBN: 978-1-84464-573-2
Ebook ISBN: 978-1-84464-574-9

Paths International Ltd
www.pathsinternational.com
Published in the United Kingdom

CPSIA information can be obtained
at www.ICGtesting.com
Printed in the USA
LVHW062038260220
648310LV00004B/6

9 781844 645732